Reconsidering Tolkien

edited by Thomas Honegger

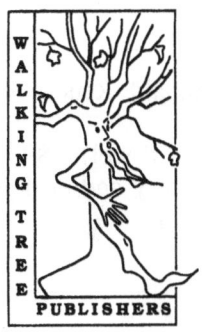

2005

Cormarë Series

No 8

Series Editors

Peter Buchs • Thomas Honegger • Andrew Moglestue

Library of Congress Cataloging-in-Publication Data

Honegger, Thomas (editor)

Reconsidering Tolkien

ISBN 3-905703-00-9

Subject headings:

Tolkien, J. R. R. (John Ronald Reuel), 1892-1973 – Criticism and interpretation
Tolkien, J. R. R. (John Ronald Reuel), 1892-1973 – Language
Fantasy fiction, English - History and criticism
Middle-earth (Imaginary place)
Literature, Comparative.

All rights reserved. No portion of this book may be reproduced, by any process or technique, without the express written consent of the publisher.

Preface

The main part of this volume dates back to the ESSE[1] 7 session on 'Reconsidering Tolkien' held at Zaragoza in September 2004. The seminar had been initiated by Eva Müller-Zettelmann (University of Vienna) who could, unfortunately, not attend. Jan Frans van Dijkhuizen (University of Leiden), acting as co-convenor, kindly asked me to take over and chair the session. The contributions by Natasa Tucev, Dirk Vanderbeke, Martin Simonson, Guillermo Peris and Eduardo Segura, and myself are based on papers presented in this seminar. Marion Gymnich, who had also been announced with a paper at the conference, could not attend but was nevertheless able to contribute to this volume. The remaining contributions resulted from an additional call for papers and were selected for inclusion by the board of editors.

Thomas Honegger
Jena, Spring 2005

---

[1] ESSE stands for *European Society for the Study of English* and is the biggest European association for university teachers of English language and literature.

to JP

Table of Contents

Marion Gymnich
Reconsidering the Linguistics of Middle-earth:
Invented Languages and Other Linguistic Features
in J.R.R. Tolkien's *The Lord of the Rings*   7

Eduardo Segura and Guillermo Peris
Tolkien as Philo-Logist   31

Thomas Honegger
Tolkien Through the Eyes of a Mediaevalist   45

Paul E. Kerry
Thoughts on J.R.R. Tolkien's
The Lord of the Rings and History   67

Natasa Tucev
The Knife, the Sting and the Tooth:
Manifestations of Shadow in *The Lord of the Rings*   87

Jean-Christophe Dufau
Mythic Space in Tolkien's Work
(*The Lord of the Rings*, *The Hobbit*
and *The Silmarillion*)   107

Dirk Vanderbeke
Language, Lore and Learning
in *The Lord of the Rings*   129

Martin Simonson
The Lord of the Rings in the Wake of the Great War:
War, Poetry, Modernism, and Ironic Myth   153

Connie Veugen
'A Man, lean, dark, tall':
Aragorn Seen Through Different Media   171

Reconsidering the Linguistics of Middle-earth: Invented Languages and Other Linguistic Features in J.R.R. Tolkien's *The Lord of the Rings*[1]

MARION GYMNICH

Abstract

The languages of Tolkien's *The Lord of the Rings* have always fascinated scholars and other readers. Peter Jackson's film trilogy also picks up many of the linguistic devices and themes one encounters in the novel. The article seeks to explore the effects created by the linguistic evocations and the metalinguistic reflections both in the novel and in the films. The paper discusses the effects produced by the invented languages, which have played a particularly prominent role in linguistic approaches to Tolkien. Moreover, further linguistic aspects of *The Lord of the Rings*, such as linguistic variation on the regional, social, and individual level, reflections on the nature and origin of language, and the association of language with magic, will be addressed.

THE FASCINATION OF THE LANGUAGES IN *THE LORD OF THE RINGS*

The fact that J.R.R. Tolkien's *The Lord of the Rings* presents a considerable number of words, sentences, and even entire songs in languages invented by the author continues to fascinate scholars, 'ordinary' readers and, recently, moviegoers. Elizabeth Kirk (1971:10) describes the linguistic achievement of Tolkien's novel as follows:

> Tolkien has created an entire world in its spatial and chronological dimensions, peopling it with languages which have, in a necessarily stylized and simplified

---

[1] I am very grateful to Alexandre Segão Costa and Sara B. Young for their enormously helpful comments on an earlier version of this paper.

version, all the basic features of language, from writing systems and sound changes through diction and syntax to style.

In a similar vein, Ruth Noel (1980:6) argues that "the languages are certainly not random. They lend Tolkien's works a unique dimension of realism." Although the opinion that *The Lord of the Rings* is a work of linguistic genius has not gone unchallenged,[2] there appears to be a fairly widespread consensus among literary critics and linguists that the foregrounding of language is a crucial element of Tolkien's novel.[3] Thus it is not surprising that there are numerous articles dedicated to the language(s) of *The Lord of the Rings*. Most of these have been written by scholars who, like Tolkien himself, are linguists and medievalists, and many of them draw upon the tools provided by historical linguistics in their discussion of Tolkien's fictional linguistic creations, exploring the (pseudo-) etymologies of words in the Elvish languages Sindarin and Quenya, applying phonological principles such as Grimm's Law to the invented languages, or charting the relationships between the languages of Middle-earth. There are even grammars and dictionaries of Tolkien's invented languages.[4] Peter Jackson's film trilogy (2001-2003) also suggests that linguistic considerations constitute an integral part of Tolkien's Middle-earth, since the films pick up many of the linguistic features and themes of the novel and even increase the use of the in-

---

[2] See Kirk (1971:6): "It is certainly the case that the style is the main (or at least the overt) bone of contention between the enthusiasts and those who declare they could not get past the first twenty pages."

[3] See, for example, Algeo (2001:250), who claims that "Tolkien's linguistic and onomastic inventiveness was indeed epic in proportions", and Honegger (2004:3), who argues that "the foundation of Tolkien's world is basically linguistic."

[4] See, for instance, the grammars and dictionaries compiled by Noel (1980), Kloczko (1995), Derdzinski (2000), Kloczko (2002), Baixauli (2003), Krege (2003), Pesch (2003), and Pesch (2004).

vented languages considerably.[5]

In an attempt to reconsider the linguistic aspects of Tolkien's creation the present paper seeks to explore the effects created by the linguistic evocations and by the metalinguistic reflections in Tolkien's novel as well as in the film trilogy. Any study of the linguistic features of *The Lord of the Rings* and their potential impact on the reader/viewer has, of course, to take into consideration the invented languages, in particular the prominent Elvish languages, Dwarvish, Rohirric, and Black Speech. But there are also other remarkable linguistic and metalinguistic aspects of Tolkien's novel, which so far have generated less interest among critics: references to linguistic variation (on the regional, social and individual level) and other features which suggest that the reader is confronted with authentic speech communities; reflections on the nature and origin of language; and the association of language with magic, which can be traced back to genres like the fairy tale, but which has also interesting implications for the 'linguistics of Middle-earth'.

THE AESTHETICS OF LANGUAGE(S) AND IMPLICIT CHARACTERIZATION BY MEANS OF LANGUAGE

Most of the invented words and sentences in *The Lord of the Rings* are attributed to the Elves, and it is generally accepted that Tolkien regarded the Elvish languages as the core of his fictional creation.[6] Thus, it is hardly surprising that the languages of the Elves have attracted much of the attention devoted to the linguistic features of *The Lord of the Rings* and have given rise to a considerable amount of linguistic investigation

---

[5] The extended versions available on DVD, however, contain significantly more scenes that are interesting from the point of view of linguistics than the cinematic versions.

[6] Thomas Honegger (2004:2) observes: "The linguistic history of Elvish has been relatively well researched, not least since the Eldarin tongues were at the centre of Tolkien's preoccupation with invented languages and the extant corpus of Elvish offers sufficient material for linguistic-philological inquiries."

and speculation.[7] Although the publications on the Elvish languages suggest that the invented languages might appeal in special ways to the linguist (in particular the historical linguist), one can assume that the use of the invented languages also has a significant impact on the linguistically uninitiated reader (and viewer). First of all, as was already pointed out in the introduction, the invented languages can be seen as an authentification strategy, since they lend the fictional world additional complexity and verisimilitude.

Moreover, all of the invented languages in *The Lord of the Rings* contribute to the construction of the fundamental 'otherness' of the cultures they are associated with. Given the frequency of words and sentences in Elvish, one could argue that it is in particular the otherness of the Elves that is established linguistically. Their languages, which are incomprehensible to the reader, enhance the air of mystery surrounding these immortal creatures and their ancient civilization. This effect is also achieved in the films, which feature a number of dialogues in Elvish (generally translated into English by means of subtitles). The films, however, additionally use the visual track to emphasize the 'otherness' of the Elves, for instance by showing them surrounded by white light in some scenes. The soundtrack and the visual track thus corroborate each other to set the Elves apart from the other races in Middle-earth.

Elvish is used quite extensively in the film trilogy. In fact even the very first words viewers hear in *The Fellowship of the Ring*, namely the first lines of the commentary from the off spoken by actress Cate

---

[7] It has, for example, repeatedly been argued that the Elvish language Quenya was constructed by Tolkien to resemble Finnish, whereas Sindarin has been described as resembling Welsh, at least in terms of its phonology (see, e.g., Noel 1980, Doughan 1993, Keene 1995, Algeo 2001). For the purposes of the present paper it is not necessary to distinguish between the different Elvish languages. It is often only the information provided in the Appendix to *The Lord of the Rings* and not the story itself that allows the reader to infer which of the Elvish languages is used in a particular situation. In the film, the notion that there are different Elvish languages is not introduced at all.

Blanchett, who plays the Elf Galadriel, are in Elvish (and are then apparently translated into English).[8] The novel, in contrast, features the first sentence in Elvish only after about a hundred pages, in a dialogue between Frodo and a group of Elves. By introducing the viewers immediately to the history of the rings and by confronting them with Elvish, the film trilogy right from the beginning stresses the mysterious and the extraordinary.[9] The fact that the Elvish lines in the opening sequence are whispered – in contrast to what seems to be their English 'translation' – and the solemn music accompanying these lines are both aspects of the soundtrack that add to the air of mystery. Since the first part of the commentary from the off is spoken while the screen is still black, the viewers' attention is inevitably drawn even more to what is said, and thus the soundtrack may unfold its full potential.

An examination of the situations in which Elvish is spoken in the novel and in the films also throws an interesting light on how Elvish is likely to be seen by the readers/viewers. In the novel, the Elvish languages are used in songs and poems – something that stresses their role as carriers of Elvish culture. Yet, Elvish is also shown to be a conventional means of communication; it is clearly not reserved for ritual functions or formal occasions, but seems to be a living language fulfilling the complete range of functions a language may have. The films pick up this complex role of Elvish. Thus, the viewer gets the impression that the language(s) can be used for virtually any kind of communication, since there are a number of dialogue passages in Elvish. Yet, especially in the

---

[8] The first words in English are taken over from the novel, where they appear in a completely different context, though, and are not associated with the Elves and their languages. They are spoken by the Ent Treebeard after the war is over and the Ring has been destroyed: "[...] the world is changing: I feel it in the water, I feel it in the earth, and I smell it in the air." (Tolkien 1983:1017)

[9] The much more down-to-earth opening section of the novel – "Concerning Hobbits" – is picked up only in the extended filmic version, where it is inserted *after* the scenes depicting the history of the rings.

first film of the trilogy, *The Fellowhip of the Ring*, Elvish is also associated quite strongly with magic: When Arwen makes the river rise to protect Frodo from the Ringwraiths she does this by means of an incantation in Elvish.[10] Just like in the opening lines, the mystery evoked by the use of Elvish is supported by sound effects, by a filtering of the actress's voice. When Legolas says a prayer in Elvish (*The Two Towers*) or when Aragorn sings a song in Elvish during the coronation ceremony (*The Return of the King*), the situations also suggest that Elvish is used for ritual functions. Even when characters exchange greetings in Elvish, there are overtones of the ritualistic.

In addition to contributing to the notion of the 'otherness' of the cultures created in *The Lord of the Rings*, the differences between the various invented languages are also meant to establish cultural differences. The underlying assumption clearly is that the aesthetic qualities of a language (or the lack thereof) indicate how civilized its speakers are. The Elves, representatives of an ancient civilization, are portrayed as possessing extraordinary dignity and grace. In the films, this idea is expressed in the visual track for example by showing the elegant and elaborate Elvish clothes, which are very different from the Hobbits' rustic clothes. In the novel, metalinguistic comments on the Elvish languages also transport the idea that the Elves are aesthetically and culturally superior to the other inhabitants of Middle-earth. Aragorn at one point says about a song translated from Elvish that it is "'in the mode that is called *ann-thennath* among the Elves, but is hard to render in our Common Speech, and this is but a rough echo of it'" (Tolkien 1983:210). The 'Common Speech', the *lingua franca* used by Men, Hobbits, and even Orcs in Middle-Earth, obviously cannot compete with Elvish as far as its aesthetic qualities are concerned.

---

[10] In the novel, the river also rises and thus protects Frodo and the reader may come to the conclusion that this results from Elvish magic, but there is no incantation in Elvish.

It is hardly surprising that invented languages such as Dwarvish and in particular the Black Speech of Mordor fare even worse than the Common Speech in the aesthetic comparison with the "sweet syllables" (Tolkien 1983:254) of Elvish, which in a song fall "like clear jewels of blended word and melody" (Tolkien 1983:254).[11] The language of the Orcs is referred to as "'hideous'" (Tolkien 1983:345) and "abominable" (Tolkien 1983:466); it sounds "at all times full of hate and anger" (Tolkien 1983:466), and when an Orc speaks the Common Speech, he makes it "almost as hideous as his own language" (Tolkien 1983:466). There is only one longer sample of the Orc language in the novel: "'*Uglúk u bagronk sha pushdug Saruman-glob búbhosh skai*'" (Tolkien 1983:466). Further examples are provided by names, for example Grishnákh, Uglúk, Gorbag, Lagduf, Muzgash, Shagrat. When Gandalf reads out loud the inscription on the One Ring, which represents the Black Speech of Mordor,[12] the words bring about a drastic change in the wizard's voice and inspire terror, demonstrating very clearly the power of language to affect people aesthetically and emotionally: "The change in the wizard's voice was astounding. Suddenly it became menacing, powerful, harsh as stone. A shadow seemed to pass over the high sun, and the porch for a moment grew dark. All trembled, and the Elves stopped their ears." (Tolkien 1983:271)[13] The terrible impact of the Black Speech on all present is also depicted very effectively in the film, where the menace inherent in Black Speech is additionally expressed by

---

[11] It is a well-known fact that Tolkien meant the Elvish languages to be aesthetically pleasing. See the discussion in Honegger (2004:3-4).

[12] "'*Ash nazg durbatulûk, ash nazg gimbatul, ash nazg thrakatulûk agh burzum-ishi krimpatul.*'" (Tolkien 1983:271)

[13] See also Stanton (2001:154): "On the Ring, the language of Mordor has become a symbol of both power and evil. It is meant to be perceived as a language of surpassing ugliness, and its ugliness is just the audible equivalent of its evil. Harsh menace is in its very tones, and hearing it becomes a way of understanding, as Gandalf implies, how dreadful Middle-earth will be under the dominion of its chief speaker."

the fact that it seems to echo in Frodo's mind, with the words of the inscription repeated not by Gandalf but by Sauron himself.

The aesthetic juxtaposition of the different languages, which serves as an index of the cultural and even moral differences between their speakers, is highlighted by means of sound symbolism, or, to put it more precisely, by language-specific preferences for certain sounds and sound combinations. In the Elvish languages there are, for example, many mid and front vowels as well as nasal consonants,[14] whereas in the language of the Orcs back vowels, bilabial and velar plosives ([p], [b], [k], [g]), and the palatal fricative (represented by <sh>) are particularly prominent.[15] It goes without saying that the aesthetic qualities ascribed to the languages on the part of the author and, presumably, the reader/viewer are highly subjective; still, it can be assumed that the individual reader's/viewer's preferences for certain sounds and sound sequences are strongly influenced by his/her native language, by its sounds and sound sequences, since these influence what sounds familiar or even 'possible' to the reader/viewer. The sequence [zg], for example, which appears three times in the inscription on the Ring (in the word *nazg*), is not among the sound sequences that are possible in English and is thus bound to be perceived as 'outlandish'.

Dwarvish clearly resembles the language spoken by the Orcs and Black Speech, and metalinguistic comments also throw a relatively negative light on this language. When Sam hears Gimli pronounce some place names in Dwarvish, the Hobbit remarks: "'A fair jaw-cracker dwarf-lan-

---

[14] See the following samples of Elvish: "'*Elen síla lúmenn' omentielvo*'" (Tolkien 1983:94); "*Ai na vedui Dúnadan! Mae govannen!*" (Tolkien 1983:226); "*noro lim, noro lim, Asfaloth!*" (Tolkien 1983:239); "*dún-adan*" (Tolkien 1983:249); "*A Elbereth Gilthoniel, silivren penna míriel o menel aglar elenath! Na-chaered palandíriel o galadhremmin ennorath, Fanuilos, le linnathon nef aear, sí nef aearon!*" (Tolkien 1983:254); "*Arwen vanimelda, namarië!*" (Tolkien 1983:371).

[15] Hyde (1987) provides a detailed analysis of sound symbolism in *The Lord of the Rings*.

guage must be!'" (Tolkien 1983:303) In *The Lord of the Rings* there are few samples of Dwarvish – several place names, such as Khazad-dûm (Tolkien 1983:257), Baraz (Tolkien 1983:300), Zirak (Tolkien 1983:300), Shathûr (Tolkien 1983:300), and Bundushathûr (Tolkien 1983:300), as well as Gimli's battle-cry: *"Baruk Khazâd! Khazâd aimênu!"* (Tolkien 1983:557). In the extended film version of *The Fellowship of the Ring*, Gimli, moreover, says something in Dwarvish to the Elf Haldir. The viewers are not told what Gimli says, but the situation, Gimli's dislike of Elves, and especially Aragorn's comment "That was not so courteous" suggest that the rough language was used to convey a rude content – something that goes very well with Tolkien's overall aesthetic approach to languages.[16] Still, though the Dwarves are certainly rough, they are definitely not uncivilized, let alone evil, and Gimli is presented very positively. This at least partially counterbalances the aesthetic-elitist overtones of Tolkien's approach to languages. Dwarvish shows that a language that is perceived as aesthetically unpleasant does not necessarily have to evoke evil or a lack of civilization; there is thus after all no simplistic one-to-one relationship between the aesthetic qualities of a language and the characteristics of its speakers in *The Lord of the Rings*, although, as Stanton (2001:154) argues, "[t]he moral quality of the languages of Middle-earth is one of their benchmarks."

The language spoken by the inhabitants of Rohan is somewhat different from the other invented languages – both in terms of its linguistic roots and as far as its effects are concerned. The fragments representing this particular language are clearly reminiscent of Old English rather than being purely imaginary. Words such as *éored* (e.g. Tolkien

---

[16] The language of the Dwarves, just like Elvish, is surrounded with an air of mystery, since the dwarves have a secret language "that they teach to none" (Tolkien 1983:324). See also Gimli's explanation of the word *mithril*: "For here alone in the world was found Moria-silver, or true-silver as some have called it: *mithril* is the Elvish name. The Dwarves have a name which they do not tell." (Tolkien 1983:335)

1983:455, 862, 868, 869, 1001) or *mearas* (e.g. Tolkien 1983:456, 531) are genuine Old English lexemes. The sentences "'*Westu Théoden hál!*'" (Tolkien 1983:540), which, as Honegger (2004:16) points out, "echoes Beowulf's greeting to Hrothgar", and "'*Ferthu Théoden hál!*'" (Tolkien 1983:545), "which is easily recognisable as Old English (Mercian?)" (Honegger 2004:16), also evoke Old English. These fragments "give the book an archaic flavor" (Irwin 1987:46), and they suggest much more concrete cultural associations than the other languages in *The Lord of the Rings* – at least for those readers who recognize the references to Old English.[17] The allusions to the Anglo-Saxon culture contribute to the portrayal of Rohan as an archaic warrior culture: "'They are proud and wilful, but they are true-hearted, generous in thought and deed; bold but not cruel; wise but unlearned, writing no books but singing many songs, after the manner of the children of Men before the Dark Years.'" (Tolkien 1983:451) The film trilogy significantly increases the depiction of Rohirric by providing a short but impressive scene in the extended version of *The Two Towers* in which Éowyn sings a dirge in what is quite clearly Old English. Both the language and the vocal performance of the song in this scene convey a strong archaic flavour.

The language of Rohan can also be placed within the 'aesthetic ranking' of languages that is established by metalinguistic comments in *The Lord of the Rings*. When Gimli and Legolas hear Aragorn sing a song in Rohirric, which neither of them understands, they are struck by the "strong music" (Tolkien 1983:530) of the language. Legolas, moreover, characterizes the language as being "'like to this land itself; rich and rolling in part, and else hard and stern as the mountains'" (Tolkien

---

[17] See Honegger (2004:16): "Tolkien's description of the Riders of Rohan contains too many historical and cultural parallels to the Anglo-Saxons as to make it likely that his choice of Old English was motivated merely by linguistic convenience." See also Algeo (2001: 251).

1983:530). Whether this sounds like an adequate description of Old English or not is up to the reader's judgment. At any rate, Rohirric is apparently deemed aesthetically pleasing by the Elf, though its appeal is different from that of the 'sweet syllables' of Elvish.

LINGUISTIC VARIATION

The "unique dimension of realism" (Noel 1980:6) that language lends to *The Lord of the Rings* also results from the fact that the languages are shown to be synchronically variable. This aspect of the linguistic universe of *The Lord of the Rings* is much more noticeable in the novel than in the film. Readers of the novel are, for example, informed that the Elves do not speak a uniform language but instead different dialects and even languages ("the speech that the Silvan folk east of the mountains used among themselves was unlike that of the West", Tolkien 1983:360). The Orcs also speak different languages and dialects; the Orc tribes even have to use the Common Speech as *lingua franca* among themselves, because they speak mutually unintelligible languages: "To Pippin's surprise he found that much of the talk was intelligible; many of the Orcs were using ordinary language. Apparently the members of two or three different tribes were present, and they could not understand one another's orc-speech." (Tolkien 1983:466)[18]

Linguistically, the Hobbits at first sight seem to be the least interesting group. Their way of speaking is very close to the reader's language, which is in line with the general tendency to invite the reader to adopt the Hobbits' perspective.[19] Yet, there are a number of linguistic

---

[18] See also: "As usual, they [a group of Orcs] were quarreling, and being of different breeds they used the Common Speech after their fashion." (Tolkien 1983:960)

[19] Cf., for example, Kehr (2003:16), who emphasizes that the Hobbits' speech resembles the readers' way of speaking much more than the speech of the other groups of speakers in Middle-earth. In the Appendix to *The Lord of the Rings* ("On Translation") it is pointed out that, though the text has been translated from the 'real' language of the Hobbits, which is not English, "the whole of the linguistic setting has

features which emphasize that the Hobbits constitute a speech community with its own conventions and traditions. Tolkien quite clearly suggests that there is a certain amount of regional and social variation within the Hobbit speech community – something that adds to the complexity of the linguistic universe created in *The Lord of the Rings*.[20] For example, both in the novel and in the first film of the trilogy the gatekeeper at Bree guesses that Frodo, Sam, Merry, and Pippin are from the Shire as soon as he hears them speak, which implies that there is a certain amount of regional variation: "'Hobbits! Four Hobbits! And what's more, out of the Shire by their talk,' said the gatekeeper" (Tolkien 1983:167). There is also an explicit reference to "the Bree-dialect" (Tolkien 1983:171).[21] Given the fact that Tolkien's novel indicates that there is regional variation within the Hobbit speech community, Pippin's Scottish accent in the film trilogy does not seem to be completely out of place in Tolkien's Middle-earth, though the novel certainly offers no basis for this particular dialect or even for Pippin's portrayal as speaker of a regional dialect that distinguishes him from Frodo and Merry.

While regional variation is only established indirectly, i.e. by means of metalinguistic remarks, social variation within the Hobbit speech community is much more noticeable. The utterances of Hobbits belonging to a low social class display features such as a departure from the usual pattern of subject-verb agreement or double/multiple negative

---

been translated as far as possible into terms of our own times" (Tolkien 1983:1167), with the Hobbits serving as the reference point for the reader and thus as the speakers of modern English.

[20] The varieties have been traced back to different real-world models. Johannesson (1997) identifies the Hobbit dialect as a dialect in Oxfordshire and Warwickshire. Borgmeier (1982:406, n.23) sees parallels between the Hobbit lower class sociolect and Cockney.

[21] Note that the remark that the words 'history' and 'geography' are not "much used in the Bree-dialect" (Tolkien 1983:171) says more about the lack of education among the Bree-Hobbits than about any linguistic differences.

constructions. These features are extremely common in English lower class sociolects[22] and thus invite the reader to allot literary characters using these features a place in the social hierarchy. The most prominent speaker of a non-standard variety is certainly Sam, who, as his sociolect emphasizes, is socially inferior not only to Frodo, but also to Merry and Pippin, whose utterances, in the novel at least, largely correspond to Standard English. In Sam's speech there is often no third person singular inflection (e.g. "'It don't seem", Tolkien 1983:100; "It don't look", Tolkien 1983:302); instead, there is an ungrammatical first person or second person singular affix -*s* (e.g. "you comes", Tolkien 1983:631). Moreover, he sometimes uses double negatives (e.g. "we don't see nothing", Tolkien 1983:380; "there ain't no", Tolkien 1983:673), and there are some lexical sociolectal features (e.g. "coney", Tolkien 1983:679, 680; "taters", Tolkien 1983:680). Some of the other Hobbits in the Shire and in Bree, for example Farmer Maggot and the servant Bob, speak the same sociolect. Even the innkeeper Barliman Butterbur, who is not a Hobbit but a Man, uses very similar constructions.[23] The presentation of sociolects in *The Lord of the Rings* thus indicates or at least stresses social differences between the characters and at the same time creates an impression of verisimilitude, of 'linguistic realism'.

The verisimilitude of the Hobbit speech community is further enhanced by the notion that there exist distinct communicative rules and traditions within this community, such as specific linguistic taboos, proverbs and fixed expressions. In his birthday speech, Bilbo violates one of the linguistic taboos of the Hobbit speech community when he

---

[22] See, for example, Trudgill (1999:125): "Most non-standard dialects of English around the world permit multiple negation."

[23] Butterbur uses multiple negatives in the following complaint: "'I haven't got six legs, nor six eyes neither!'" (Tolkien 1983:169) See also: "Then I couldn't find nobody" (Tolkien 1983:183). In addition, he does not use the third person singular -*s*, as the following utterance shows: "'If he don't come, ring and shout!'" (Tolkien 1983:170)

refers to the total number of his guests as 'one Gross', thus using an expression in a totally inappropriate context, as the reader is told: "The invitations [to Bilbo's party] were limited to twelve dozen (a number also called by the Hobbits one Gross, though the word was not considered proper to use of people)" (Tolkien 1983:40). The reaction of the guests indicates that they are fully aware of Bilbo's violation of a taboo: "*Your numbers were chosen to fit this remarkable total: One Gross, if I may use the expression.* No cheers. This was ridiculous. [...] 'One Gross, indeed! Vulgar expression.'" (Tolkien 1983:42) Hobbits appear to have quite a number of proverbs and fixed expressions, such as "'*Short cuts make long delays,*'" (Tolkien 1983:101), "*Strange as News from Bree*" (Tolkien 1983:166), "*news from Bree*" (Tolkien 1983:673), "*sure as Shiretalk*" (Tolkien 1983:673), "what in the Shire" (Tolkien 1983:107, 113).[24]

In addition to alluding to regional and social varieties, which reinforces the idea that there are complex speech communities in Middle-earth, Tolkien also creates idiolects, that is idiosyncratic linguistic features associated with a single character. This is particularly obvious with Sméagol/Gollum, whose speech shows a number of idiosyncrasies. It was already pointed out above that Tolkien uses sound symbolism to characterize the various speech communities depicted in *The Lord of the Rings*. The same principle may also apply on the level of individual characters, as the linguistic presentation of Gollum shows. On the sound level, his way of speaking is marked by a predominance of the voiceless alveolar fricative [s], which often is even doubled in the written representation to

---

[24] Proverbs and fixed expressions also seem to be characteristic of other speech communities in Tolkien's Middle-earth. In Gondor, for example, proverbs seem to be quite common: Boromir, for example, says "'when heads are at a loss bodies must serve, as we say in my country'" (Tolkien 1983:309), obviously drawing upon a fixed expression, and Faramir muses "*Night oft brings news to near kindred*, 'tis said." (Tolkien 1983:691)

convey the idea that Gollum's utterances sound very much like hissing, as the following example illustrates:

> 'Ach, sss! Cautious, my precious! More haste less speed. We musstn't rissk our neck, musst we, precious? No, precious – *gollum*! [...] We hate it,' he hissed. 'Nassty, nassty shivery light it is – sss – it spies on us, precious – it hurts our eyes. [...] Where iss it, where iss it: my Precious, my Precious? It's ours, it is, and we wants it. The thieves, the thieves, the filthy little thieves. Where are they with my Precious? Curse them! We hates them.'
> (Tolkien 1983:638)

The association with hissing, with the sounds produced by a snake, the quintessential, Biblical embodiment of evil, supports the portrayal of Gollum as sly, treacherous, and dangerous. Yet, while his articulation clearly recalls the hissing of a snake, his choice of words at times is reminiscent of speech associated with children, for example when Gollum addresses the Hobbits as "sleepy heads" (Tolkien 1983:660) or "sleepies" (Tolkien 1983:728).

The peculiarities of the inflectional morphology in Gollum's utterances also show remarkable similarities with the grammatical characteristics of the English produced by children at an early stage in the process of first language acquisition. Like many children acquiring their first language, Gollum departs from the rules for subject-verb agreement. These departures from standard grammar might alternatively be read as reflecting the character's social background. But Gollum also produces ungrammatical plural forms in a manner that does not evoke a sociolect but rather the overgeneralization of a regular inflectional rule – a phenomenon one sometimes observes in children's English.[25] Gollum fre-

---

[25] On overgeneralization in the process of first language acquisition, see, for example, Radford (1990:25): "[...] the occurrence of overgeneralized forms like *two mans*

quently attaches the plural suffix *-(e)s* to forms that are already marked as plural, either by the regular plural suffix or because they are irregular plural forms. This gives rise to constructions such as "Hobbitses" (Tolkien 1983:639), "mices" (Tolkien 1983:639), "Orcses" (Tolkien 1983:640, 653), "snakeses" (Tolkien 1983:652), "wormses" (Tolkien 1983:652), "carrotses" (Tolkien 1983:680), "trickses" (Tolkien 1983:723). On the one hand, the additional plural affixes increase the number of [s]-sounds in Gollum's speech, thus reinforcing his hissing. On the other hand, such ungrammatical forms are reminiscent of the speech of children at the early stages of first language acquisition. From the point of view of the reader, Gollum is thus linguistically positioned between the association with a snake (evil) and the naivety of a child – an ambivalence that correlates with his behaviour, both in the novel and in the film, since he at least temporarily seems to waver between treachery and a childlike trust in his 'Master' Frodo. Even Gollum's tendency to refer to himself with his name instead of using the pronoun 'I', which in the film is quite clearly seen as being indicative of schizophrenia, is a common feature of the early stages of first language acquisition. As far as Gollum's idiosyncratic use of personal pronouns ('we' and 'they' instead of 'I') is concerned, however, the text clearly privileges an interpretation as schizophrenia.

LANGUAGE PHILOSOPHY IN MIDDLE-EARTH

The sections of *The Lord of the Rings* that deal with the living trees, the Ents, and in particular with the Ent Treebeard, "'the oldest living thing that still walks beneath the Sun upon this Middle-earth'" (Tolkien

---

and *two peoples* in early child speech is generally taken as very strong evidence that children 'know' that +s is a noun inflection [...]. However, although forms like *mans* and *peoples* demonstrate acquisition of the plural +s morpheme, they clearly do not demonstrate mastery of it."

1983:520), contain reflections on the nature and on the origin of language. Treebeard tells the Hobbits Merry and Pippin that the Ents were taught to use language by the Elves, who were the first beings in Middle-earth to develop a language: "'Elves began it, of course, waking trees up and teaching them to speak and learning their tree-talk. They always wished to talk to everything, the old Elves did.'" (Tolkien 1983:489) Despite the fact that the Ents received the gift of language from the Elves, Entish does not appear to have much in common with the Elvish languages. The main characteristic of Entish seems to be the enormous length of its words, whereas the Elvish languages are "'quickworded'" (Tolkien 1983:499) in comparison. The length of Entish words is not accidental, but results from the Ents' philosophy of language, their concept of the relationship between language and the world.

According to the Ents, the words of a language ought to reflect the nature of the entities they denote. Thus, Ents apparently do not conceive of words as linguistic signs in the Saussurian sense, namely as *arbitrary* connections of a signifier and a signified. Instead, the Ents assume that the relationship between signifier and signified should be motivated. Since Entish words even reflect the *history* of the entities they denote, linguistic signs in Entish have to be inherently instable, perpetually growing longer as the entities they refer to become older. The Ent Treebeard thus has a much longer real name, reflecting his long life span, as he explains to the Hobbits Merry and Pippin: "'[...] my name is growing all the time, and I've lived a very long, long time; so *my* name is like a story. Real names tell you the story of the things they belong to in my language, in the Old Entish as you might say.'" (Tolkien 1983:486) Words in the Common Speech, being very short in comparison to Entish words, thus cannot but appear inadequate to the Ents: "Treebeard repeated the words thoughtfully. '*Hill*. Yes, that was it. But it is a hasty word for a thing that has stood here ever since this part of the world was shaped.'" (Tolkien 1983:487) The Entish philosophy of language as a reflection of reality apparently also implies the possibility that words may become shorter when what they refer to is fading away: "'[...] *Laurelindórenan*! That is what the Elves used to call it, but now they make the name shorter: *Lothlórien* they call it. Perhaps they are right: maybe it is fading, not growing.'" (Tolkien 1983:488) The enormous length of words in Entish is emphasized by the following sample of Entish, which, as Treebeard points out, is merely *part* of a word: "'*a-lalla-lalla-rumba-kamanda-lind-or-burúmë*'" (Tolkien 1983:486).

The sample of Entish, in contrast to the other invented languages in *The Lord of the Rings*, looks very much like gibberish. Yet, it also recalls the apparently meaningless strings of sounds produced by Tom Bombadil, whose magic power the readers are familiar with from previous chapters. The similarity between Entish and Tom Bombadil's speech may be grounded in the fact that they are the oldest creatures in Middle-earth, which suggests that their languages might express ancient ways of thinking and of relating to the (natural) world that cannot be captured by more 'modern' languages. This interpretation is supported by the fact that the Ents did not take over the 'hasty'/'modern' languages of the Elves, who taught the Ents to speak, but developed their own, very different language instead. The unusual nature of Tom Bombadil's utterances is even explained directly as resulting from the fact that they represent "an ancient language whose words were mainly those of wonder and delight" (Tolkien 1983:162).

LANGUAGE AND MAGIC

In *The Lord of the Rings* language appears in many different forms. One of the basic ideas even seems to be that virtually everything in nature is capable of speech. In Middle-earth not only the treelike Ents, but also animals are endowed with the gift of language, even if their languages are understood by few others. The inhabitants of Bree believe that the Rangers "understand the languages of beasts and birds" (Tolkien

1983:165), and the wizards Gandalf and Radagast also communicate with animals. In the fictional universe of Middle-earth, which is highly charged linguistically, it seems almost inevitable that language may become a powerful instrument in the service of both good and evil forces, or, as Noel (1980:57) puts it, "[t]he languages of Middle-earth retained a vital power. The right user or the right words could unleash significant powers for good or for evil." This aspect of language becomes, for example, apparent when the companions try to open the door leading into the mines of Moria, which "'nothing will move [...] save the spell of command'" (Tolkien 1983:324). The notion that the power inherent in language is tied to an exact rendering of particular words is of course familiar to the readers of fantasy literature and, in particular, of fairy tales; it is the very principle behind the idea of magic spells. The specific treatment of language in *The Lord of the Rings* thus can also be traced back to the tradition of the fairy tale.[26]

The Elvish languages, as "the linguistic embodiment of good" (Meile 1997:219), show certain protective powers. Frodo instinctively uses Elvish words as a protective charm when he is attacked by the Ringwraiths on Weathertop. When Aragorn tries to heal Frodo after the attack, he sings "a slow song in a strange tongue" (Tolkien 1983:214), which, no doubt, is an Elvish language. In Mordor both Frodo and Sam instinctively utter words in Elvish that offer some kind of protection, even without knowing what they are saying (Tolkien 1983:747, 756-57, 949). Tom Bombadil's songs, which often seem to be mere gibberish, a "long string of nonsense-words" (Tolkien 1983:134), constitute an even more powerful instance of language in the service of protective magic. This mysterious, ancient inhabitant of Middle-earth twice uses his songs to rescue the Hobbits from great danger.

---

[26] Cf. Paul Nolan Hyde (1983:11), who emphasizes that "Tolkien's intention was not to write a realistic or post-realistic novel but to write instead a fairy tale in the classic sense."

The idea that language can be associated with an enormous power also surfaces in linguistic taboos. In Gondor, Sauron apparently is not referred to with his name, as the following utterances by Boromir and Faramir suggest: "'I have heard of the Great Ring of him that we do not name'" (Tolkien 1983:260), "'in the beginning of Gondor, when He whom we do not name was overthrown'" (Tolkien 1983:697). This taboo suggests that "[b]y naming a thing, it is given power and can become a reality" (Keene 1995:8). Thus, Aragorn tells Pippin not to utter the name of Mordor (Tolkien 1983:202) and admonishes Frodo when the latter jokes that he is losing so much weight that he might ultimately turn into a Ringwraith (Tolkien 1983:201). The notion of linguistic taboos, which can be encountered quite frequently in fairy tales, also explains why the Hobbits are warned that it may be dangerous to reveal one's own name. Even Treebeard believes that giving away one's real name is potentially dangerous (Tolkien 1983:486). The fear of the power of language and in particular of revealing one's name is apparently also shared by Sauron ("'Neither does he use his right name, nor permit it to be spelt or spoken,' said Aragorn", Tolkien 1983:436). The Hobbits, however, do not seem to share this attitude towards language; they do not worry about referring to themselves or to evil things and beings by their real names, thus exhibiting a 'modern', non-magical view of the relationship between language and reality.

Several representatives of the evil forces in *The Lord of the Rings* harness the power inherent in language for their purposes. The wizard Saruman has achieved particular mastery of the use of speech to exert power. He is an expert at manipulating others, at putting a spell on them by the power of his voice. As soon as the spell is broken the victims are typically unable to recall the exact words or even explain the power of the words in any rational way: "Those who listened unwarily to that voice could seldom report the words that they heard; and if they did, they wondered, for little power remained in them" (Tolkien 1983:601).

The speech of other evil creatures in Middle-earth is equally elusive. For example, Frodo feels that the eerie shrieking of the Ringwraiths transmits words which are incomprehensible to the Hobbits: "'It was not bird or beast,' said Frodo. 'It was a call, or a signal – there were words in that cry, though I could not catch them'" (Tolkien 1983:104). In the Old Forest, the Hobbits are haunted by the impression that the trees speak to each other, "passing news and plots along in an unintelligible language" (Tolkien 1983:125). When the willow-tree in the Old Forest puts a spell on the Hobbits, lulling them asleep, natural sounds seem to change into words: "They shut their eyes, and then it seemed that they could almost hear words, cool words, saying something about water and sleep. They gave themselves up to the spell and fell fast asleep at the foot of the great grey willow." (Tolkien 1983:132). The boundary between mere sounds/noise and language, a systematic way of expressing meaning by means of linguistic signs, is blurred. In a similar manner, the song of the evil barrow-wights only slowly turns into an intelligible text:

> Suddenly a song began: a cold murmur, rising and falling. The voice seemed far away and immeasurably dreary, sometimes high in the air and thin, sometimes like a low moan from the ground. Out of the formless stream of sad but horrible sounds, strings of words would now and again shape themselves: grim, hard, cold words, heartless and miserable. [...] After a while the song became clearer, and with dread in his heart he [Frodo] perceived that it had changed into an incantation (Tolkien 1983:156).

What the speech used by many of the evil creatures seems to have in common is that it is elusive, unintelligible, at least at first, and at the same time enormously powerful. This plays on the fear of the unknown and emphasizes the enigmatic nature of the power of language.

CONCLUSION

An exploration of the manifold ways in which *The Lord of the Rings* addresses linguistic issues shows very clearly that linguistic devices and metalinguistic comments constitute an integral part of the architecture of Tolkien's work. They contribute significantly to the portrayal of the different characters and cultural groups of Middle-earth, and they are connected with the core issue of the conflict between good and evil. In his treatment of language(s) Tolkien draws upon knowledge provided by the academic discipline of linguistics, but also on the tradition of the fairy tale. Thus, the approach to language in *The Lord of the Rings* combines the 'realistic' and the 'magical'. It may be this mixture of the realistic and the magical in the treatment of language that accounts for the fascination exerted by the language(s) of *The Lord of the Rings* – a fascination that is not limited to the novel, but that translates very well into Peter Jackson's film trilogy.

MARION GYMNICH holds a Ph.D. in English from the University of Cologne. Currently, she is coordinator of the International Ph.D. Programme in Literary and Cultural Studies at Justus Liebig University, Giessen. She is the author of *Entwürfe weiblicher Identität im englischen Frauenroman des 20. Jahrhunderts* (2000) and *Grundkurs Anglistische Sprachwissenschaft* (1998, together with Jon Erickson) as well as of a number of articles on women's writing, postcolonial literature, the interface between literature and linguistics, and narrative theory (unreliable narration, multiperspectival narration, possible-worlds theory, feminist/gender-oriented narratology, narratological approaches to audiovisual media). She has edited *Literature and Linguistics: Approaches, Models, and Applications. Studies in Honour of Jon Erickson* (2002, together with Ansgar Nünning and Vera Nünning), *Literatur – Erinnerung – Identität: Theoriekonzeptionen und Fallstudien* (2003, together with Astrid Erll und Ansgar Nünning), and *Funktionen von Literatur: Theoretische Grundlagen und Modellinterpretationen* (2005, together with Ansgar Nünning).

References

ALGEO, John, 2001, 'A Fancy for the Fantastic: Reflections on Names in Fantasy Literature', in *Names* 49.4, 2001, pp. 248-253.

BAIXAULI, Luis González, 2003, *La lengua de los Elfos,* Barcelona: Ediciones Minotauro.

BORGMEIER, Raimund, 1982, 'No Message? Zur Deutung von Tolkiens *The Lord of the Rings*', in *Anglia* 100, 1982, pp. 397-412.

DERDZINSKI, Ryszard, 2000, *Gobeth en Iham Edhellen/Sindarin Dictionary*, Katowice: Gold Maggot Publishers.

DOUGHAN, David, 1993, 'Elvish and Welsh', in *Mallorn* 30, 1993, pp. 5-9.

HONEGGER, Thomas, 2004, 'The Westron Turned into Modern English: The Translator and Tolkien's Web of Languages', in HONEGGER, Thomas (ed.), 2004, *Translating Tolkien: Text and Film*, Zurich, Berne: Walking Tree Publishers, pp. 1-20.

HYDE, Paul Nolan, 1983, 'Translations from the Elvish: The Linguo-Cultural Foundations of Middle-Earth', in *Publications of the Missouri Philological Association* 8, 1983, pp. 11-16.

HYDE, Paul Nolan, 1987, 'Quenti Lambardillion: A Column on Middle-earth Linguistics', in *Mythlore* 14, 1987, pp. 57-62.

IRWIN, Betty J., 1987, 'Archaic Pronouns in *The Lord of the Rings*', in *Mythlore* 14, 1987, pp. 46-47.

JOHANNESSON, Nils-Lennart, 1997, 'The Speech of the Individual and of the Community in *The Lord of the Rings*', in BUCHS, Peter and Thomas HONEGGER (eds.), 1997, *News from the Shire and Beyond – Studies on Tolkien*, Zurich, Berne: Walking Tree Publishers, pp. 11-47.

KEENE, Louise E., 1995, 'The Restoration of Language in Middle-earth', in *Mythlore* 20, 1995, pp. 6-13.

KEHR, Eike, 2003, *Die wiederbezauberte Welt: Natur und Ökologie in Tolkiens* The Lord of the Rings, Wetzlar: Förderkreis Phantastik in Wetzlar e.V.

KIRK, Elizabeth D., 1971, '"I Would Rather Have Written in Elvish': Language, Fiction and *The Lord of the Rings*', in *Novel* 5, 1971, pp. 5-18.

KLOCZKO, Edouard, 1995, *Dictionnaire des langues Elfiques, volume 1. Quenya – Français – Anglais*, Toulon: Tamise Productions.

KLOCZKO, Edouard, 2002, *Dictionnaire des langues des Hobbits, des Nains, des Orques et autres créatures de la Terre du Milieu, de Númenor et d'Aman*, Argenteuil: A.R.D.A.

KREGE, Wolfgang, 2003, *Elbisches Wörterbuch*, Stuttgart: Klett-Cotta.

MEILE, M.G., 1997, 'Sauron's Newspeak: Black Speech, Quenya, and the Nature of Mind', in Rauch, Irmengard and Gerald F. Carr (eds.), 1997, *Semiotics around the World: Synthesis in Diversity*, Vol. 1, Berlin: Mouton de Gruyter, pp. 219-222.

NOEL, Ruth S., 1980, *The Languages of Tolkien's Middle-earth*, Boston: Houghton Mifflin.

PESCH, Helmut W., 2003, *Elbisch: Grammatik, Schrift und Wörterbuch der Elben-Sprache von J.R.R. Tolkien*, Bergisch-Gladbach: Bastei-Lübbe.

PESCH, Helmut W., 2004, *Elbisch: Lern- und Übungsbuch der Elben-Sprachen von J.R.R. Tolkien*, Bergisch-Gladbach: Bastei-Lübbe.

RADFORD, Andrew, 1990, *Syntactic Theory and the Acquisition of English Syntax*, Oxford: Blackwell.

STANTON, Michael N., 2001, *Hobbits, Elves, and Wizards*, New York, Houndmills, Basingstoke: Palgrave Macmillan.

TOLKIEN, J.R.R., 1983, *The Lord of the Rings*, London: Unwin.

TRUDGILL, Peter, 1999, 'Standard English: What It Isn't', in BEX, Tony and Richard J. WATTS (eds.), *Standard English: The Widening Debate*, London, New York: Routledge, pp. 117-128.

Tolkien as Philo-Logist

EDUARDO SEGURA AND GUILLERMO PERIS

Abstract

John Ronald Reuel Tolkien taught not only Anglo-Saxon and History of the English Language at the universities of Leeds and Oxford, but he was also a writer. Some think that, not being a 'professional' writer of fiction, he made many mistakes in the composition of his narratives. Yet the question arises, what 'professional writer' really means in this context. A producer of best-sellers maybe? If so, he was a great professional indeed. Many others think that the first one hundred or so pages of *The Lord of the Rings* are especially 'heavy' or 'hard reading'. However, it is not the purpose of this paper to analyse the reason of this lack of appreciation for the taste of words – which is what Tolkien mainly attempted. We will try rather to explain why, to many readers, Tolkien, and specially *The Lord of the Rings*, makes difficult reading – despite the fact that, to many of them, his are *the books*. That is why we will explore Tolkien's concept of the mythic, narrative value of words.

Professor Tolkien was deeply convinced of the way he had helped Philology to step forward. His mythic creation (*sub-creation*, in his own words) was the result of many years of study and reflection on the principles of language. Was it possible to create, to tell a story, according to those principles? Could words *really* create a world? Tolkien thought that Philology was the crossroads where his talent as storyteller, the long years devoted to the science of words, and the love and delight for the sound or *euphony* of words met. Back in 1911, he had envisaged a vast epic poem in the hope that he could dedicate it to England, his beloved country.

At the age of 7 he had already invented some languages on his own. Words had the music of Music to him. Eventually, he became knowledgeable in about seventeen languages and dialects, some of which he could also speak fluently. He also invented at least five languages as the framework for his own creation. The 'inner consistency of reality' that he wanted for his 'secondary worlds'[1] should come from the viability of those languages as vehicles of culture, as tools to construct a feasible world, where anything could *really* happen.

He called that synthesis between Philology – a real *love for words* to Tolkien – and artistic writing *sub-creation*. Sub-creation should explain the cumulative world view formed by any given culture expressed by a language. Secondly, a philologist should rescue the historical sense of words. To sub-create a world means, to Tolkien, to re-create the past through the history of a language.

In his farewell speech to the Oxford faculty at the end of his academic career, Tolkien referred to the triumph of a 'misologist' point of view over his field of study. He was, of course, referring to the fact that the programme of English Studies he had opposed, consisting in a sharp distinction between literary criticism on the one hand, and language studies on the other, had ousted his own programme of 'Lit. and Lang.' as the components of a single discipline called 'Philology'. As Tolkien saw it, the study of literature and language stemmed from an undifferentiated love for words that, in his opinion, the current syllabus abandoned. Beyond the factual articulation of his discipline, what really saddened him was the picture or convictions about language that emerged as a consequence of its divorce from literature. This is why he calls the point of view responsible for the new programme 'misologist'. In other words, we may assume that, for Tolkien, the way we study literature nowadays is evidence of a 'hate of words'. Indeed, our notions concerning language

---

[1] For an explanation of the notions of 'secondary world' and 'secondary belief', see Tolkien's essay "On Fairy-Stories" (Tolkien 1964:44-52, *passim*).

have changed *together* with our notions about literature – in itself a very telling development.

Modern readers thought it impossible to utter coherently, and convincingly, in *our* age, through *our* language, something like *The Lord of the Rings*. Tolkien had his own professionally informed convictions about literality, metaphor, and Logos with relation to language that we have largely abandoned. As a consequence, and *in this order*, he had a notion about literature that we have long abandoned too: literature as myth, because – for Tolkien – ours is a mythic grammar.[2] We have ruled out many of the possibilities or aspects of language, literature, and experience that *The Lord of the Rings* proves 'feasible'.

If we trust Tolkien, the story of *The Lord of the Rings* 'grew in the telling', but as a consequence of the invented languages, since these pre-existed Middle-earth. Tolkien, first and foremost, wanted a language capable of saying "a star shines on the hour of our meeting" with full meaning. Why an Elf should choose to use precisely 'light' and 'star' as a means to express joy is made clear by the story of *The Silmarillion*. For Frodo and Gildor, no matter how fixed, the expression is not a trope, but has quite literal, historical echoes. Stars play a role in the plot of *The Lord of the Rings*, because they are part of the structure of Middle-earth that its dwellers use to define their existence. An Orc could never have employed a star in his expression of joy in a greeting, for the word and the reality of a star has a completely different meaning for him. As for light, the reality expressed by the word is such a fundamental element in Middle-earth that it alone becomes a literal weapon against Shelob, as we will see.

In other words, Elves choose the reality that defines their stand-

---

[2] See "On Fairy-Stories" (Tolkien 1964:24-25) concerning the power of adjectives as a sub-creative tool.

point on creation through the use of this expression. The elements used in it are a clue to their past and to the extent to which that race values the elements themselves. Tolkien devised Middle-earth in such a way that, for the Free Peoples, what is at stake in the struggle involves the literal preservation of light in their world, and through it, the presence of its ultimate source. The world of *The Lord of the Rings* is given its rules of existence by a pre-existing linguistic expression.

This is only one example of how Tolkien's philological mind worked. He first thought of the language, and then made a world that fulfilled the meaning of the expression – its extent. In other words, he made a world that was commensurate with the possibilities of a language, a world that lived up to what the language was capable of expressing.

But why did he in the first place want a language to express meaningfully a content like the one expressed in Frodo's greeting? Probably because he felt that to express it in modern English would be to drain reality from the expression, because many readers would take it as a trope, a figure of speech, florid rhetoric – in a pejorative sense. Language and Logos mirror each other. We tend to think that an expression like Frodo's, if linguistically understandable, adds nothing to our understanding of the world, to the Logos as we have learned to construe it in modern times. Hence, it has probably merely rhetoric value for modern day English speakers. It puts forth a disposable, unreal piece of information according to our outlook, and therefore, within modern English, it occupies the marginal territory of figure of speech. Our Logos is not commensurate with the possibilities of our language for there are words that 'fall outside' our predominant notions of reality. If only for this, we are almost certain that he would consider our modern outlook and its concomitant reflection in modern English to be rather 'misologist' realities. Tolkien loved words too much to deny them meaningful possibilities.

Now, Tolkien was not only in love with Philology. His way to an understanding of this world was philological. The beginning of Fantasy was the word – any word. The world was created through the Word and in the Word (see Gen. 1, and John 1, 1-18).[3] That means that the humus of his inspiration was not personal but linguistic, *philo-logical*. So that, as Humphrey Carpenter has pointed out, the way he reacted when confronted with a contradiction was not "that's not what I want; I should change it" but "that's not so; I must discover why". Tolkien wrote according to the *forma mentis* of a historian, of a philologist – a historian of words and meanings. He was not *only* a novelist.[4]

Why, then, is writing 'fiction' or, even worse, 'fantasy' not 'escapism' to Tolkien? Because he was convinced, as a philologist, that every literature has as an inevitable reference a specific way of thinking, which is expressed through a language. In *The Lord of the Rings* we can find many characters whose mentality as members of a race is explained through linguistic resources.[5]

Middle-earth is coherent with how it is spoken about. It has the coherence of a coherent language. We understand the *notion*, say, of a talking tree, but it is not consistent, coherent speech as applied to our world. Tolkien made a world where a talking tree was coherent and credible, following the capacity of language to mix the two concepts very much like a metaphor is a device that unites incompatible concepts.

As Verlyn Flieger points out, "what is metaphorical for us is literal

---

[3] In the world created by Tolkien, *Eä!* is the word that Ilúvatar pronounces to give existence to his thought, the initial Music. See *The Silmarillion*, especially the first chant, the "Ainulindalë".

[4] See Segura (2004:34).

[5] See Galadriel's *Namárië!*, or the reaction of Gimli when he looks upon the Kheled-zâram after Gandalf's death in the mines of Moria. Treebeard is the best example of Tolkien's philological mind turned into a character. In our opinion the shepherd of trees is Tolkien walking through the woods – naming the world, and so recalling it.

in *The Lord of the Rings*" because Tolkien made a world where our metaphors are capable of existing. Their impossibility for our world (precisely the impossibility that makes them metaphors) is turned into coherence for the other world. The author did not need to think of a 'never-never land', only of the 'other-worldly' capacity of our language: its all too familiar capacity for metaphor. We fiddle with Fairyland every time we use a metaphor because, literally speaking, what a metaphor expresses is unlikely in literal terms in the actual world as we know it. If metaphors are understandable, in spite of this, it is because our language is part of a 'mythic grammar'.

The paradox is this: it is very difficult to understand literal reality without the aid of a supposed world of non-factual possibilities, because reality is not literal, univocal, but polysemic.

As Mardones explains, "everything that exists is worded". So that a philologist knows reality, and not only the words, as a means to access true knowledge of the world. "Reality is present to us weighed down with ambiguity" because the world is essentially polysemic.[6] That is, it is always newly expressed, and so it is not possible to run out the ways to name it.

From the point of view of Tolkien's poetics, and according to his notion of sub-creation, *mythopoeia* is understood as a process of *retelling* the world: only through stories can we recover the cosmological sense of this world. Fantasy is the mirror where reality becomes fully coherent. For Tolkien, Fantasy cannot be utterly unreal – and therefore not 'escapist' – in the same sense in which metaphors cannot be considered 'false language'. Rather, both can be explained as projected reality. Similar to language, a myth recreates and interprets the conditions of

---

[6] This notion has been explained by E. Segura and G. Peris in their preface to *Tolkien o la fuerza del mito: la Tierra Media en perspectiva* (Segura and Peris 2003:17).

existence, the conditions under which life is experienced. Myths, not being bound to factual immediacy, project worlds that are stripped of immediacy and are given the internal (narrative) cohesion of reality, thus making possible numberless applications – i.e., interpretations. Myths, then, exhibit one of the most fundamental aspects of reality as seen from Tolkien's philological mind: they are (and have been) endlessly utterable, endlessly interpretable: ambiguous.

Languages re-create (*sub-create*) shared reality, like myths do. As Verlyn Flieger explains, languages are for Tolkien a process of "splintered light" in which each language, like every myth, speaks truthfully in its own manner, accommodates or reflects reality in its own way, shedding light while recreating it. From this point of view, Tolkien, *as philologist* in the root sense of 'lover of words' was bound to refer to his artistic activity as *sub-creation*, because the act of employing a language is envisioned as a sub-creative act: the rationale of language itself empowers us as sub-creators of reality, which is to say, 'mythmakers', 'storytellers'.

Ultimately, this is the reason that explains Tolkien's deep dislike of allegory. Allegory necessarily implies an impoverishment of meaning, and more importantly, an intellectually rachitic *experience* of this world, since there is no chance to live it and look at it through the light of myth – the 'invented' worlds, from Latin, *'invenire'* –, that allows a reencounter of this world as the discovery of a new land that was, however, old – familiar:

> I cordially dislike allegory in all its manifestations, and always have done so since I grew old and wary enough to detect its presence. I much prefer history, true or feigned, with its varied applicability to the thought and experience of readers. I think that many confuse 'applicability' with 'allegory'; *but the one*

> *resides in the freedom of the reader, and the other in the purposed domination of the author.*
> (Tolkien 1982:11, "Foreword" to *LotR*; emphasis added)

As C.S. Lewis puts it, concerning *The Lord of the Rings*:

> What shows that we are reading myth, not allegory, is that there are no pointers to a specifically theological, or political, or psychological application. A myth points, for each reader, to the realm he lives in most. It is a master key; use it on what door you like. [...] That is why no catchwords as 'escapism' or 'nostalgia' and no distrust of 'private worlds' are in court. This is [...] sane and vigilant invention, revealing at point after point the integration of the author's mind. [...] As for escapism, what we chiefly escape is the illusions of our ordinary life.
> (Lewis 1982:85)

Chesterton wrote that in William Shakespeare's *Hamlet*, it is not the prince who changes: it is me who change as I read the story – and always will. Hamlet is a myth, and so, eternal. Myth is potentially infinite in its applicability. The question is not 'What can we find from the author in the story?' – as myth –, but 'What does this myth teach me about myself through the ages?' Classics are classics because they do not depend on a personal projection of the psyche. They are universally applicable.

Every character in *The Lord of the Rings* is capable of such an analysis. Historical wisdom in Middle-earth is updated through lore. Each character treasures an atavistic wisdom, a *micro-history* that illuminates the present of the story from the past of history. At times, the words are breathed by the characters not knowing what they really mean. It is pure metaphor born from an emotional need to express a feeling which is beyond hope and tears – and joy:

> Frodo gazed in wonder at this marvellous gift that he had so long carried, not guessing its full worth and potency. Seldom had he remembered it on the road, until they came to Morgul Vale, and never had he used it for fear of its revealing light. *Aiya Eärendil Elenion Ancalima!* he cried, and knew not what he had spoken; for it seemed that another voice spoke through his, clear, untroubled by the foul air of the pit.
> (*LotR* p. 747)

In the same way, at a crucial moment of the quest Sam Gamgee asks himself and his master about the meaning of stories, considering the possibility of being himself part of an unfinished tale – a very Tolkienian notion. And Aragorn tells Éomer at the time of their first meeting about the powerful image of grass as a matter of legend.

In this context, psychological theories on myth make a valiant attempt to defend its validity, but they reduce the natural ambiguity of reality to a mere one-to-one correspondence. They try to build an archetypal explanation of the world, so that the individual instances are seen only as examples of the eternal return in Nature. Joseph Campbell and his hero of a thousand faces are a good example of this trend. Tolkienian applicability is rooted in the freedom of the reader and, at the same time, in that quality of reality that we referred to: polysemy.

Modern notions about myth (Jung, Lacan, Campbell) have often stressed the direct relationship between myth and the *psyche* (individual and collective), as if myths were a transformed symbolic language of deep unconscious processes. Out of this conviction comes the still frequent practice of assuming that specific mythical elements correspond to specific mental structures in a virtually one-to-one process: A as symbol *is* B as mental structure. This turns myth into an allegorical narration, something against which Tolkien protested because of his philological outlook on myth and its implications on knowledge through language – that is, the relationship between logos and language. We think he could not help but to see in this psychologically based method an attempt to make univocal what his discipline had shown him to be essentially polysemic, that is, infinitely expressible: reality, and myth as its most life-like projection.

The limit of this psychological explanation turns into a process of self-knowledge. A philologist should protest against that mentality since myth is, to him, expression of reality: splintered light, illumination. Characters are not the mask, or some sort of a portrait of the author. They themselves speak to us about their joy, anguish, fears, and hopes. As we find in *The Lord of the Rings*, C.S. Lewis wrote:

> Anguish is, for me, almost the prevailing note. But not, as in the literature most typical of our age, the anguish of abnormal or contorted souls: rather that anguish of those who were happy before a certain darkness came up and will be happy if they live to see it gone. [...] Nostalgia does indeed come in; not ours nor the author's, but that of the characters. [...] In the Tolkienian world you can hardly put your foot down anywhere from Esgaroth to Forlindon or between Ered Mithrin and Khand, without stirring the dust of history. (Lewis 1982:86)

It is Treebeard's anguish and nostalgia for the Ent-wives that makes the reader feel that something from a golden, happier age, is now lost, gone beyond hope. His grief shines over the reader's, as he tries to grasp the shadow of an impossible bliss.

Tolkien was not only in love with Philology: the way he related to the world was through Philology. The discipline mediated between his mind, and the world. It was his bridge to the Logos. More importantly, this also applies for the 'fictional' characters, and very coherently so: "for the whole vast sweep of his mythology is in truth just that – the exploration of the implications and ramifications of the one word *Eä*" (Flieger 2002:57). That is, how each language sub-creates (or recreates) this command: how each language says *Eä* through its peculiar way of understanding creation, how each language is a creative version of creation.

The Lord of the Rings helps us to understand the transmission of wisdom that travels through literary tradition. We understand that in the origin of language, of speaking, there is a myth – the need to express and *retell* the world. Our grammar is mythic. Tolkien achieved that feeling of a feasible, credible world, as a positive chance of the mind. He worded an 'asterisk reality', as T. Shippey puts it: he sub-created it.

In Middle-earth 'willing suspension of disbelief' is not needed; credibility shines through the plot. It is 'secondary belief' as an assertion. There is no hidden truth, or imitation of the factual world we live in. It is not a negative 'enchantment' or 'magical' way of thinking – and therefore, false. We perceive that reality is so wonderful when looking at it in the mirror of myth, once again, as for the first time. Thus we can see in it the multiplicity of meaning which is the main characteristic of this world – the *real* one. What is magical is *this* world, not Fairyland; and it is a world that can only be told through the magic spell of mythic language, the lore, or lógos, or mythos.

Perhaps we, as readers of the 21st century, are one with the characters of *The Lord of the Rings*. This is so because in a world in which myths are synonymous with nursery rhymes, perhaps interesting but ultimately superseded, unreliable representations of truth, we lack a term that fits a tale in which characters wholly made up of 'the stuff of the imagination' engage in actions, thoughts, and quests that can be a more adequate medium to convey a moving and intelligent gloss about our condition precisely because these actions and thoughts are consistent with their imaginary world.

For, despite *The Lord of the Rings*' obvious applicability to our reality, nowadays "we *must* call this book 'fantasy' – with obvious implications as opposed, for example, to 'novel' – for lack of another word" (Flieger 2002:57-58). Our most immediate cultural heritage does not provide a word. It does not provide a fitting word because it does not have too much experience with a work like *The Lord of the Rings* – perhaps a few more by Tolkien himself.

As a relation of means (unashamed 'fantasy') and possible ends (far reaching hermeneutic knowledge of our present condition) *The Lord of the Rings* is literally unprecedented. We can describe its components, but their effect is perhaps more serious than we have learned to expect from them. Tolkien may have conveyed similar perplexities in his fictional world. We find ourselves as Pippin in Denethor's hall trying to find the words that would do justice to something hobbits know little about. Or Bilbo in Smaug's lair, a sight which left him 'breathless', 'literally'. Or like Éomer who thinks that Tolkien's insightful depiction of the relation between language and Logos is, because of its inclusion within a 'legend', suitable for the realm of Faërie only.

We may say, therefore, that his presuppositions are closer to home than what we are inclined to believe from an author of 'fantasies'. The journey from his fantastic creation to its foundations in the sources of our worldly, everyday language seems at first unlikely, but – as Tolkien has demonstrated – possible, feasible; and ultimately, true.

EDUARDO SEGURA, PhD in Philology, teaches at the Universidad Católica San Antonio, Murcia (Spain). He has written two books on Tolkien: a biographical sketch titled *J.R.R. Tolkien, el mago de las palabras* (Casals, 2002), and *El viaje del Anillo* (Minotauro, 2004), which is based on his doctoral dissertation. He has also edited, with Guillermo Peris, *Tolkien o la fuerza del mito: la Tierra Media en perspectiva*, a translation of the Tolkien 1992 Centenary Conference Proceedings. esegura@pdi.ucam.edu

GUILLERMO PERIS, BA in Philology, is currently working on his doctoral dissertation, concerning the Modernist notion of 'myth'. He is, together with Eduardo Segura, co-editor of the INKLINGA collection for LibrosLibres publishers. His next publication will be a study on New Formalism in critical context. willperis@ono.com

References

FLIEGER, Verlyn. 2002. *Splintered Light: Logos and Language in Tolkien's World*. Second edition. First edition 1983. Kent, Ohio: The Kent State University Press.

LEWIS, C. S. 1982. "Tolkien's *The Lord of the Rings*". In *On Stories and Other Essays on Literature*. Ed. by Walter Hooper. New York: HarcoutBraceJovanovich.

SEGURA, E. 2004. *El viaje del Anillo*. Barcelona: Minotauro ediciones.

SEGURA, EDUARDO and GUILLERMO PERIS (eds.). 2003. *Tolkien o la fuerza del mito: la Tierra Media en perspectiva*. Madrid: LibrosLibres.

TOLKIEN, J.R.R. 1964. "On Fairy-Stories". In *Tree and Leaf*. London: HarperCollins, pp. 9-70.

TOLKIEN, J.R.R. 1982. *The Lord of the Rings*. London: Unwin Hyman.

Tolkien Through the Eyes of a Mediaevalist

THOMAS HONEGGER

Abstract[1]

The Lord of the Rings, ever since its publication, has been something of a nuisance to traditional literary critics and has been maligned often and with zest. The main reason for these strong – and often irrational – reactions are primarily due to the fact that *The Lord of the Rings* does not fit into the literary mainstream and challenges standard critical assumptions about what a work of twentieth-century fiction should be like. The standard tool-kit of the literary critic seems utterly inadequate. Mediaevalists, in contrast, have often taken a more sympathetic view of Tolkien's work. My contribution will therefore present several 'mediaeval' approaches towards Tolkien, evaluate their critical value and discuss their contribution towards a more adequate understanding of Tolkien's literary work.

INTRODUCTION

All roads lead to Rome, or so it is said. The roads to Middle-earth and to Tolkien are not as numerous, but the last few decades of Tolkien criticism have shown that there exists a wide variety of approaches towards understanding Tolkien's work. The 'interpretatio mediaevalia', i.e. the explanation and exploration of Tolkien's work with the help of mediaeval studies, is one of them and, as I will argue, not the least one. It claims that a working knowledge of the various mediaeval languages and familiarity with mediaeval culture and literature is indispensable for the appreciation of Tolkien's work. The ideal mediaevalist would possess

---

[1] I would like to thank Allan G. Turner PhD for his knowledgeable comments and helpful suggestions. A German version of this essay was published in *Hither Shore*.

expertise in all the different European national languages and cultures. These 'ideal mediaevalists', however, are few and far between, while the ever-increasing specialisation in academia has led to subdivisions and restrictions. Being the product of the European academic system, I too suffer from these limitations and I will therefore restrict myself to the Anglicist mediaevalist's point of view.

Michael Drout, in his study *Beowulf and the Critics by J.R.R. Tolkien* (published 2002), propagates the 'interpretatio mediaevalia' (without explicitly labelling his approach) and provides the following characterisation:

> The single best way to understand and appreciate Tolkien's fiction is to become literate in medieval literature. Optimally, one would learn Anglo-Saxon and Old Norse and Latin and read the many works that T.A. Shippey and others have shown to be the sources of Tolkien's world. (Drout xiii)

A truly ideal training programme for future Tolkien experts – and like so many ideal things, it has hardly ever been attained in this world. Professor Drout is, as one may have guessed, a mediaevalist of the Anglicist persuasion and therefore biased in favour of the 'interpretatio mediaevalia'. Thus, before proceeding, I would like to present briefly some other important approaches and see whether the 'interpretatio mediaevalia' is indeed the ideal way to Tolkien's work.

CRITICS

The literary works published during Tolkien's lifetime (1892-1973), i.e. *The Hobbit, The Lord of the Rings, Smith of Wootton Major, Farmer Giles of Ham* and *The Adventures of Tom Bombadil*, are, with the possible exception of *The Homecoming of Beorhtnoth, Beorhthelm's*

Son,[2] read, understood and enjoyed by a large non-mediaevalist audience. Most people seem to be happy without an 'interpretatio mediaevalia' – indeed, without any interpretation at all, whether literary or otherwise.

Things are different with literary critics, i.e. those persons who deal with literature professionally. With them the need for 'explanation' has been great, all the more so since *The Lord of the Rings* in particular has proven resistant to easy classification by means of the usual criteria and critical categories. As a result, *The Lord of the Rings* has been the victim of much (and often acerbic) critical abuse, which is more an expressions of the literary critics' frustration and inability to come to terms with it than a sign of any inherent flaws. It seemed for a long time that the literary tool-kit was simply not adequately equipped for dealing with such a work. In recent years, however, critics such as Tom Shippey (*J.R.R. Tolkien: Author of the Century*, 2000) and Brian Rosebury (*Tolkien. A Cultural Phenomenon*, 2003) have successfully begun to explore the relationship of *The Lord of the Rings* to the dominant literary modes of the first half of the 20th century – notably that of modernism. Tolkien's work, according to Shippey and Rosebury, can be best understood, like modernism, as a reaction to the prevailing cultural and economic situation. Such a re-evaluation of Tolkien's major literary work is, in my opinion, a promising approach and will, hopefully, further the understanding of the peculiarities of *The Lord of the Rings* so that it need no longer remain an erratic in the literary landscape of the 20th century.

It is not only the extraordinary literary characteristics of *The Lord of the Rings* that have attracted the attention of the critics. Since

---

[2] *Beorhtnoth* does not seem to fit in very well with the other titles. After all, it was originally published not as a literary work, but in *Essays and Studies* (1953). It appeared as 'literature' in Tolkien's lifetime only in the American *The Tolkien Reader* (1966). Yet in the original article Tolkien refers to it as 'poem' and in 1954 a radio production of *Beorhtnoth* was performed on the BBC Third Programme.

the mid-60s at the latest, we have had the situation that predominantly literary critical disdain has gone hand in hand with overwhelming (popular) public acclaim, which has found expression in numerous Tolkien societies and fan clubs. Confronted with the 'Tolkien phenomenon' both critics and admirers have been looking for explanations and, maybe correctly, have begun to turn towards the person of the author in search for answers.

TOLKIEN THE MAN

The unexpected success of *The Lord of the Rings* generated a lasting interest in the 'man behind Middle-earth' – not least since most of the mythological framework, of which the narrative gave only tantalising glimpses, remained for a long time inaccessible to the audience, so that Tolkien was the only person who could grant access to the wider realms of Arda. Although Tolkien proved to be a conscientious correspondent (see the selection of letters edited by Humphrey Carpenter with the assistance of Christopher Tolkien, which appeared in 1981 as *The Letters of J.R.R. Tolkien*), the great majority of readers had to wait till Christopher Tolkien published *The Silmarillion* in 1977 and thus provided the necessary 'mythological' background to *The Lord of the Rings*.

Tolkien himself took a critical stance towards the contemporary tendency to focus on the author and to neglect the work itself. He wrote in one of his letters: "[...] I object to the contemporary trend in criticism, with its excessive interest in the details of the lives of authors and artists. They only distract attention from an author's works [...]" (*Letters* 288). Consequently, he did not condone the publication of an authorised biography during his lifetime. One of the first biographies on Tolkien, Daniel Grotta-Kurska's *Architect of Middle-earth*, appeared in 1976, and one year later the 'official' biography by Humphrey Carpenter (*J.R.R. Tolkien: A Biography*) was published. Carpenter had the support of the Tolkien family and was given access to Tolkien's papers and writings. His biography is the most comprehensive study of Tolkien's life and provides fascinating insights into the author's creative processes. Today, a quarter of a century later, it still remains the unsurpassed and often mined standard biography, though of course the publication of a selection of Tolkien's letters (1981) and of the twelve volumes of *The History of Middle-earth* (1983-1996) has given access to new material that would have to be assessed and incorporated in a revised edition.

Soon after the publication of the authorised biography, various groups began to make use of and to modify the information provided by Carpenter for their interpretations of Tolkien's work. Humphrey Carpenter, being the son of Harry James Carpenter (Warden of Keble from 1955 onwards and Bishop of Oxford till 1970), did take some pains to present Tolkien's Catholicism from a neutral point of view without denying the central role of Tolkien's religious faith. During the 1990s, a Catholic 'reconquista' of Tolkien began, which found its climax in Joseph Pearce's publications of 1998 (*Tolkien: Man and Myth. A literary life.*) and 1999 (*Tolkien: A Celebration. Collected writings on a literary legacy.*). Tolkien's work, according to the more or less explicit argument of the 'Catholic' critics, can only be fully and properly understood by fellow Catholics – or by people who are intimately familiar with Catholicism. The very qualities and characteristics that make Tolkien's work, on the one hand, unique and, on the other, hard to fathom for most literary critics, have their roots in his Catholic faith.

The overwhelming popular success of Peter Jackson's film has brought Tolkien once more and with special emphasis to the attention of American (predominantly non-Catholic) Christians – with the result that the market is being flooded with books of very mixed quality that explore the 'spiritual' dimension of *The Lord of the Rings*. These studies typically stress the general Christian elements of Tolkien's work and tune down his specifically Catholic traits. Two recent examples may be mentioned. The first is a book by Mark Eddy Smith with the title *Tolkien's Ordinary Virtues. Exploring the Spiritual Themes of The Lord of the Rings*. It provides a 'pious' reading of *The Lord of the Rings* in thirty chapters. Each chapter focuses on a religious topic (humility, providence, sin, etc.), opening with a passage from *The Lord of the Rings* and concluding with some moral advice. The collection of essays edited by John G. West Jr. (*Celebrating Middle-earth. The Lord of the Rings as a Defense of Western Civilisation*.) offers better quality, though the individual contributions also concentrate on topics relevant to religion such as 'the Evil in Tolkien' etc. Almost all contributors are academics and the quality of the articles is accordingly higher than that of the book by Mark Eddy Smith, whose main qualification seems to be, according to the blurb, to have read *The Lord of the Rings* more than a dozen times.

Our next and for us most prominent interpretative approach to Tolkien, the 'interpretatio mediaevalia', must be seen parallel to and in connection with this aforementioned 'interpretatio catholica' or 'interpretatio Christiana'.

TOLKIEN THE MEDIAEVALIST AND THE 'INTERPRETATIO MEDIAEVALIA'

Tolkien achieved lasting and world-wide fame as the author of *The Lord of the Rings*, but this came relatively late in life – he was, at the time of publication in 1954/55, already 62 years old and 'Tolkienmania' began only another ten years later with the (unauthorised) publication of the ACE Books paperback edition in the United States. Tolkien saw himself primarily as a philologist, a mediaevalist and a man of letters with a somewhat peculiar hobby, rather than an author in the usual sense of the word. After doing some work for the *Oxford English Dictionary* (1919-20), he embarked on a distinguished academic career. He was first Reader in English Language (1920-24) and then Professor of English Language

(1924-25) at the University of Leeds, later Rawlinson and Bosworth Professor of Anglo-Saxon (1925-45) and Merton Professor of English Language and Literature (1945-59) at the University of Oxford. His academic work determined the way he saw himself personally and professionally. Tolkien stressed repeatedly the importance of his 'professional' study of mediaeval languages and literatures for his literary works; they provided the indispensable 'soil' into which his 'tree of tales' would sink its roots and find nourishment. The dependence on and connection with mediaeval literature is most clearly seen in those works that imitate mediaeval models, e.g. his poems in *Songs for Philologists*, or in works that resume mediaeval themes, such as his radio-play *The Homecoming of Beorhtnoth*, which is a continuation of and, at the same time, a commentary on the Old English heroic poem *The Battle of Maldon*. Individual motifs that derive from or are shared with mediaeval literature are abundant in most of Tolkien's other literary works. The theft of the cup from the dragon-hoard and its disastrous consequences in *The Hobbit*, for example, are a conscious echo of a similar passage in the Old English heroic poem *Beowulf*. Such parallels are easily discernible even for non-mediaevalist readers, provided they have read the relevant mediaeval poems in translation.

The discovery of the mediaeval sources, parallels or analogues is more difficult if and because, as so often, Tolkien adapted them skilfully or if the influence they exerted is only indirect. A merely superficial knowledge of mediaeval English (and I may add, Norse) languages and literatures is, in such cases, no longer sufficient. The hour of the expert has come.

It was in 1979, two years after the publication of *The Silmarillion* and Carpenter's Tolkien-biography, that Jane Chance, Professor at Rice University Texas, published her study *Tolkien's Art: A Mythology for England* (revised edition 2001, University Press of Kentucky). It was, next to Carpenter's biography, one of the first serious in-depth academic studies in which a scholar attempted to illustrate the indebtedness of Tolkien's literary works to the vernacular literature of mediaeval England. *Tolkien's Art* suffers, in my opinion, from interpretative weaknesses, numerous factual mistakes and minor misconceptions (e.g. Sauron is called "a fallen Vala" (*Tolkien's Art* 151) and also Gandalf is "most likely a Vala" (*Tolkien's Art* 147); Beowulf, after ruling the Geatas for 50 years, is still "a man of fifty" (*Tolkien's Art* 117) and Galadriel gives Sam "seeds of *elanor*" (*Tolkien's Art* 158)) as well as some truly 'Freudian' misprints ("Gimli is Groin's [son/heir]" (*Tolkien's Art* 151). I am not going to bore you with a list of 'obvious' factual mistakes, but in order to underpin my criticism I would like to discuss briefly one example that illustrates the importance of specialised 'mediaevalist' knowledge in order to avoid interpretative pitfalls. It is, of course, ironic that this interpretative mistake occurs in a study by a mediaevalist and has not been corrected for the new edition of 2001 – which gives me all the more reason to do so now and, as I hope, save the honour of the mediaevalists. Chance, in her discussion of *Leaf by Niggle*, calls Niggle and Parish "the angel and the beast" (*Tolkien's Art* 85). Such a crude and mistaken reduction of the two characters is hardly worth comment, not least since Tom Shippey (*Road to Middle-earth* 43) has proposed a convincing interpretation of Niggle and Parish as the creative and the practical side of Tolkien respectively. Chance goes on to interpret the voices overheard by Niggle in the darkness of the workhouse as different aspects of God (*Tolkien's Art* 97), i.e. the Old Testament (vengeful) God versus the New Testament (forgiving) Christ. Such an interpretation is not as obviously wrong as the one mentioned before and may seem sound to the average reader. It is a well-known literary technique to depict inner debates by means of personifying the different ideas and attitudes. However, mediaeval theology (and probably modern Catholic theology, too) and mediaeval literature would feel very uneasy with multiple 'split' divine personalities. The Christian God constitutes the trinity of God Father, God Son, and Holy Ghost, yet this must not be taken as permission to see them as three independent consciousnesses. The German translation of 'Trinity', i.e. 'Dreieinigkeit' ('Three-in-one-ness'), expresses this idea much more clearly. God Father does not debate with God Son or the Holy Ghost – they share one common unified consciousness. These theological objections would not have arisen with the interpretation of the voices as the 'Daughters of God' debating in front of God Himself. The motif of the 'Four Daughters of God' (Justicia, Misericordia, Veritas, and Pax) is well-known in mediaeval literature and, in my opinion, the most likely source of inspiration for Tolkien's 'voices'. These 'Daughters of God' act respectively as prosecutor and advocate for the human soul in front of God's seat of judgment.[3] It is typically Justicia and Misericordia who come to blows; the one advocates the severe punishment of the human soul for its sins, the other pleads forgiveness and pity. Such a scenario fully and satisfactorily explains the situation as depicted in *Leaf by Niggle* and does not have to rely on the rather heterodox idea of multiple divine personalities.

Not long after, 1982 saw the publication of Professor Tom Shippey's masterful *The Road to Middle-earth* (2nd edition 1992, 3rd edition 2003), which is not only an excellent example of the 'interpretatio mediaevalia' but also one of the best Tolkien studies in general. It is not by chance that the title of his monograph alludes to John Livingston Lowe's study on the sources of Coleridge's inspirations for his poem *Kubla Khan* (*The Road to Xanadu*, published 1927). Shippey, in the tradition of Lowe, shows with great eloquence and erudition how the philological-mediaeval tradition functioned as the well-spring for Tolkien's inspiration on all levels, ranging from minute details to liter-

---

[3] See the debate between Justicia ('Rytwysnes') and Misericordia ('Mercy') in the Middle English play *The Castle of Perseverance* (manuscript c. 1440). The relevant passages are to be found in scene XXII (Eccles 95-98).

ary motifs or large-scale structural models. Shippey's study brought home the importance of the 'interpretatio mediaevalia' with great force and established the strong position of the mediaeval approach within the field of Tolkien studies. Unfortunately, it seems that Shippey's erudition and excellence have left little of importance to discover in this field. Yet even if we cannot expect new insights of similar importance, there remains plenty to do within the established areas and a 'new generation' of mediaevalists[4] is busy emulating Shippey and 'gleaning' the fields he has reaped for the first time more than two decades ago. Lastly, the archives may still hold in stock many a surprise, as Michael Drout's recent discovery of a *Beowulf* translation by Tolkien has shown.

LEVELS OF THE 'INTERPRETATIO MEDIAEVALIA'

In the following I will present some of the most popular mediaeval approaches and discuss their usefulness.

On the 'lowest' level we find individual parallels to and borrowings from mediaeval literatures and languages. It is thanks to mediaevalists that we know that the dwarves (and Gandalf) in *The Hobbit* are named after the dwarfs in the 'Dvergatal' in the *Edda*, or that the 'Golden Hall' of the Rohirrim, Meduseld, derives its name from the Old English term for 'mead-hall', 'meduseld' (to be found in *Beowulf* l. 3065). Furthermore, a mediaevalist will immediately realise that a person called Gríma, son of Gálmód, must be a rather suspicious character since 'grîma' (sb. m.)

---

[4] The 'new generation' of Anglicist mediaevalists comprises, among others, Leslie A. Donovan (University of New Mexico), Michael Drout (Wheaton College), Jonathan Evans (University of Georgia), and Andrew James Johnston (Humboldt Universität Berlin). I have listed only those people who represent (English) Mediaeval Studies on a professorial academic level and who have put Tolkien on their teaching and research agendas.

means in Old English 'mask, helmet, ghost',[5] and 'gâlmoth' (adj.) as much as 'wanton, licentious'. Examples on this 'literal' level could be multiplied almost endlessly and are especially prominent among names of persons and places. The functions of these 'mediaeval' names are, on the one hand, to provide a link to the mediaeval legends and myths and to give to the 'educated reader' a sense of déjà vu. On the other hand, they hint at the moral disposition of a protagonist or at his or her character according to the principle 'nomen est omen'.

Another level is reached with motifs that have been taken over and adapted from mediaeval literature. Thus, the way Aragorn and his companions gain access to Théoden only gradually is modelled upon the depiction of Beowulf's arrival in Denmark and his reception at Hrothgar's court. Tolkien could alternatively have invented a 'court etiquette' of his own or looked for inspiration in another culture or era. The Rohirrim are, by and large, Anglo-Saxons in temperament and culture. Yet Tolkien took some liberties and adapted the historical model to his purposes, as the prominence of horses and cavalry shows.[6] The advantages of adapting a (most likely) historical interaction pattern lie in the feeling of authenticity it evokes and in the (inter-) textual allusions it creates. In the following, I will take a closer look at how Tolkien brought into being an intricate web of (inter-)textual allusion, namely by means of adapting the Germanic ritual of 'wassailing' or drinking to someone's health.[7] The ritual of 'presenting the cup to the lord or king' is known as part of the feast depicted in *Beowulf* (ll. 612-631). The mistress of the house, in this instance Wealhtheow, the queen-consort of

---

[5] Gríma corresponds, on the one hand, to the provocating counsellor Unferth in *Beowulf*. See Rateliff (1988) for a discussion of Gríma and his mediaeval sources and analogues.

[6] The historical Anglo-Saxons knew and valued horses, of course, but they dismounted before battle and fought on foot. See the paragraph 'The horse in Anglo-Saxon warfare' in Harrison (1993:12).

[7] See Honegger (1999) for an in-depth discussion of this motif.

Hrothgar, offers a cup of wine first to the king and then to the other members of the court and Beowulf. It is a ritual designed to represent and to affirm the hierarchical structure of the court while strengthening the cohesion between its members, and shows the queen as an independently acting person. The parallels between this Germanic ritual and the drinking ritual in the chapter 'The King of the Golden Hall' are obvious:

> The king rose, and at once Éowyn came forward bearing wine. *'Ferthu Théoden hál!'* she said. 'Receive now this cup and drink in happy hour. Health be with thee at thy going and coming!' Theoden drank from the cup, and she then proffered it to the guests. As she stood before Aragorn she paused suddenly and looked upon him, and her eyes were shining. And he looked down upon her fair face and smiled; but as he took the cup, his hand met hers, and he knew that she trembled at the touch. 'Hail Aragorn son of Arathorn!' she said. 'Hail Lady of Rohan!' he answered, but his face now was troubled and he did not smile. (*LotR* 545)

Tolkien obviously wrote this passage with the older model from *Beowulf* in mind. There, it is not a young maiden that serves the wine (or in this case mead), but Wealhtheow, king Hrothgar's wife, mother of three children, and queen of the Danes – a rather matronly figure.[8] She dispenses not only refreshments and gold, but also words of wisdom and advice (cf. lines 1159-91). Unfortunately, the passage from *Beowulf* which shows closest parallels to Tolkien's account tells us only about her offering a cup to Hrothgar and the other guests, but does not give the actual words that must have accompanied the gesture. However, it is very probable that they would have been something like 'Wæs thu hal, ...'. The queen

---

8   On Wealhtheow in general, see also the in-depth study by Damico.

– or noble lady – as the dispenser of drink is probably the original model for Tolkien's depiction of Éowyn, who also addresses first the king (Théoden, her uncle), and then his guests. Not much potential for development in this context.

It is the figure of Rowena, however shadowy she appears, that provides a submerged link to the tradition of young women used by a relative (in her case Hengest, her father) to seduce and manipulate an older, powerful man (i.e. Vortigern). Rowena appears in mediaeval accounts of the conquest and settling of Britain by the Anglo-Saxon tribes.[9] She is the daughter of Hengest, one of the leaders of the Germanic tribes that began to pour into Britain after the withdrawal of the last Roman legions in 410. Hengest and his men are first, as mercenaries, in the service of Vortigern, a British leader in the south of England. Hengest plots to take over power and uses his beautiful young daughter Rowena to extend his influence over Vortigern. He has her dressed in rich clothes and presents her to Vortigern at a feast where she kneels down and offers him a cup of wine with the words – and here I follow Layamon (l. 7141): "Lauerd king wæs hæil. For thine kime ich æm uæin."[10] Of course, these words were originally not spoken in Middle English but in proto-Old English, the language of the Germanic invaders of the 5th century. Vortigern, a Celtic-speaking Briton, does not understand proto-Old English and has it translated by one of his warriors. This interpreter, according to Layamon, not only translates Rowena's words but also provides an explanatory commentary on her gestures and the meaning of her greeting. It is customary with the Saxons and other Germanic tribes to

---

[9] See Geoffrey of Monmouth's *Historia Regnum Britanniae* (Latin, c. 1138) and the vernacular versions/adaptations of Geoffrey's chronic by Wace (*Brut*, Anglo-Norman, c. 1155) and Layamon (*Brut*, Middle English, c. 1190-1215). Aurner, in her study of Hengest, offers a comprehensive overview of the various 'Wassail'-episodes.

[10] Translation: 'Lord king, may you be of good health! I am glad about your coming.'

drink to a friend's health by saying 'leofue freond wæs hail',[11] to down the wine, refill the cup and offer it to the friend, who then answers 'thrinc hail'[12] and empties the cup. The ritual concludes with the two kissing three times. Vortigern is delighted with the prospect of kissing Rowena, so they go through the 'wassailing'[13] ritual. As a consequence of this first encounter, Vortigern falls in love with Rowena, marries her, and Hengest as his son-in-law becomes the leading power behind the throne. Mediaeval chroniclers present the episode at length because it explains the (infamous) English drinking custom of 'wassailing'.

Rowena is not the only young women used by a relative to seduce and manipulate an older, powerful man. Salome is the most prominent example of this tradition, maybe because of her claim to fame as the alleged inventor of the art of strip-tease. Rowena, however, succeeds without such strenuous exercise, and Éowyn is even further removed from consciously using her charms. Yet the 'Beowulfian' mode which has so far dominated the passage in Tolkien undergoes a slight but significant change. When Éowyn addresses Aragorn with 'Hail Aragorn son of Arathorn!', which could be interpreted as a shortened rendering of the Old English 'Wæs thu hal, Aragorn Arathornes sunu!', it is no longer solely as the female head of the royal household, but also as a young, attractive maiden – as Aragorn has noticed a short while before (*LotR* 537). What is more, she is obviously falling in love with him.[14] Thus, we have a 'Rowena' element coming in at this moment. The asexual 'Beowulfian' world in *Lord of the Rings* suffers the intrusion of an ever so slight element of eroticism. No swapping of cups, no lascivious kissing

---

11 Translation: 'Dear friend, to your health!'
12 Translation: '[I] drink to your health.'
13 'Wassail' is a contraction of 'wæs hæil'.
14 The encounter between Aragorn and Éowyn had originally been designed to initiate a love-story that would end with the marriage of the two, as becomes evident from Tolkien's notes and early drafts (cf. Tolkien, *Treason* 448).

for Éowyn and Aragorn, though.[15] The only bodily contact that takes place is the (accidental?) touching of their hands which was preceded by the silent message of her shining eyes and Aragorn's innocuous answering smile, which he abandons as soon as he notices Éowyn's emotional state by the touch of their hands. He has become aware that this 'wassailing' is no longer of 'Beowulfian' nature, although Éowyn is certainly no Rowena-like seductress, and the drinking ritual is, to many 20th-century readers, reminiscent rather of the eucharist than of the sensuous 'wassailing' custom.

The importance of the incident lies in the fact that the Rowena-Vortigern story serves as a hidden contrast to the passage in Tolkien. By implicit comparison, Tolkien provides the model of a morally and ethically responsible leader. Aragorn, unlike Vortigern, has no problems resisting the sensuous 'temptation', which is not very prominent in Tolkien's account anyway. The real problem for Aragorn is how to reject Éowyn's advances as tactfully and humanly as possible[16] – because a rejection is what is called for. Thus, the emotion that poses the greatest danger to Aragorn is not lust, but pity. If he were to accept Éowyn's offer of devotion and love, he would do so out of pity.

We now turn from those instances where the mediaeval heritage has been easy to discern and take a closer look at a less obvious 'mediaeval' influence, i.e. the problem of the perception of time in Middle-earth.

---

[15] Note, however, that the 'stirrup cup' on the occasion of Aragorn's departure for the Path of the Dead is a shared one (Tolkien, *LotR* 816) and he kisses her hand upon leaving (Tolkien, *LotR* 817).

[16] Gawain, the eponymous hero of the Middle English poem *Sir Gawain and the Green Knight*, which was well known to Tolkien, faces a similar problem, as Burnley ("Style" 30) points out: "The expressed problem ([lines] 1770-75) which faces Gawain is how to reject the lady's advances whilst offering no insult, retaining her esteem, and preserving his faith to her husband."

Sam, and with him the reader, is asking himself after the sojourn in Lórien why the waxing moon suggests that they spent only a few days there. He finally shares his bafflement with his companions:

> 'It's very strange,' he murmured. 'The Moon's the same in the Shire and in Wilderland, or it ought to be. But either it's out of its running, or I'm all wrong in my reckoning. You'll remember, Mr. Frodo, the Moon was waning as we lay on the flet up in that tree: a week from the full, I reckon. And we'd been a week on the way last night, when up pops a New Moon as thin as a nail-paring, as if we had never stayed no time in the Elvish country. Well, I can remember three nights there for certain, and I seem to remember several more, but I would take my oath it was never a whole month. Anyone would think that time did not count in there!' (*LotR* 408)

Legolas then tries to explain this phenomenon:

> 'Nay, time does not tarry ever,' he said; 'but change and growth is not in all things and places alike. For the Elves the world moves, and it moves both very swift and very slow. Swift, because they themselves change little, and all else fleets by: it is a grief to them. Slow, because they do not count the running years, not for themselves. The passing seasons are but ripples ever repeated in the long long stream. Yet beneath the Sun all things must wear to an end at last.' […] ' (*LotR* 408-409)

And Aragorn concludes:

> 'But so it is, Sam: in that land you lost your count. There time flowed swiftly by us, as for the Elves. […].' (*LotR* 409)

The differing perception of time by the different species is the starting point for Verlyn Flieger's fascinating study *A Question of Time: J.R.R. Tolkien's Road to Faërie* (1997). Flieger investigates in detail the theoretical concepts on which Tolkien bases the perception of time and space in Middle-earth and illustrates his indebtedness to contemporary scientific theories and ideas. The most significant book on this topic is obviously J.W. Dunne's *An Experiment with Time* (first edition 1927; revised and enlarged third edition 1934). Tolkien, like C.S. Lewis, owned a copy of the third edition, and Dunne's ideas must have been discussed among the Inklings (Flieger 47). *An Experiment with Time* influenced other contemporary authors, too. Thus the playwright John Balderstone has one of his protagonists summarise Dunne's ideas on time and space in his play *Berkeley Square* (1929) as follows (quoted in Flieger 57):

> Suppose you are in a boat, sailing down a winding stream. You watch the banks as they pass you. You went by a grove of maple trees upstream. But you can't see them now, so you saw them in the *past*, didn't you? You're watching a field of clover now; it's before your eyes at this moment, in the *present*. But you don't know what's around the bend in the stream there ahead of you; there may be wonderful things, but you can't see them until you get around the bend in the *future*, can you? Now remember, *you're* in a boat. But *I'm* looking up in the sky above you, in a plane. I'm looking down on it all. I can see *all at once* the trees you saw upstream, the field of clover that you see now, and what's waiting for you around the bend ahead! *All at once!* So the past, present, and future of the man in the boat are all *one* to the man in the plane. Doesn't that show how all Time must really be one? Real Time with a capital T is nothing but an idea in the mind of God.

Balderstone has succeeded in rendering Dunne's scientific jargon into easily comprehensible language. He uses, instead of talking about 'Observer 1', 'Observer 2' or 'ultimate observer' etc., everyday imagery and prefers to talk about a man in a boat (corresponding to Dunne's 'Observer 1') and a man in a plane (corresponding to Dunne's 'ultimate observer'). This way he manages to communicate Dunne's concept of 'qualified' perception of time in a clear and convincing manner. Similar differences in the perception of time seem to apply to the different races of Middle-earth, as Legolas' remarks suggest. Verlyn Flieger discusses the ramifications of this question at length in her book, though they are of no further relevance for our topic.

The question of how divine beings and Eru/Ilúvatar Himself perceive time, however, is highly relevant – and, interestingly, not dealt with by Flieger. The chapter 'The Music of the Ainur' in *The Silmarillion* describes how the creation of the cosmos and the world is outlined in broad terms by the music of the Ainur. Those Ainur who decided to participate actively in the creation of Arda, i.e. the Valar, have agreed to remain within the boundaries of this world and to subject themselves to a life in time, even if they do not age or decay. They also possess, due to their participation in the Music of Creation, a knowledge of things and events to come – which is, however, not complete. They are, to use Dunne's terminology, 'observers of a higher order'. Eru/Ilúvatar, then, could be seen as the 'ultimate observer'. Only he knows about the fate of the Children of Ilúvatar, i.e. the Elves and Men, and even if the Music of Creation has to unfold 'in time', He alone perceives it all at once and in its entirety.

What, then, has this to do with the 'interpretatio mediaevalia'? Nothing – at least at first sight. Flieger has been able to explain satisfactorily the phenomenon of the differing perceptions of time by researching the theories concerning time and space prevalent in the first three decades of the 20th century and by placing Tolkien's concept in the context of the contemporary discussion. If a mediaevalist had taken on the same task, however, then a different explanation would have been offered. A mediaevalist would rely rather on Boethius than Dunne or Balderstone. Anicius Manlius Severinus Boethius (c. 470-524) was a politician and philosopher who fell from grace at the court of the Ostrogoth king Theoderic, was imprisoned and later executed. During his time on 'death row' he composed the *De Consolatione Philosophiae*, a philosophical dialogue between the first-person narrator and Lady Philosophy. Boethius' work was later translated into Old English by King Alfred the Great, into Middle English by Geoffrey Chaucer, and into early Modern English by Queen Elizabeth I, and its influence on mediaeval thinking cannot be overestimated. One of the central problems discussed in the dialogues is the question of human free will versus divine providence.[17] How is it possible for a human being to choose freely if there exists an omniscient and all-powerful God who knows the outcome of every action in advance? The answer given by Lady Philosophy is as follows:

> [...] since the state of God is ever that of eternal presence, His knowledge, too, transcends all temporal changes and abides in the immediacy of His presence. It embraces all the infinite recesses of past and future and views them in the immediacy of its knowing as though they are happening in the present. [...] For it [i.e. God's knowledge] is far removed from matters below and looks forth at all things as though from a lofty peak above them. (Book V, §6, Watts 134)

Lady Philosophy is not, as yet, familiar with aeroplanes, but her "and looks forth at all things as though from a lofty peak above them" expresses the same idea. Tolkien's conception of time and space was certainly influenced by Dunne's theory. Yet Dunne in turn (unwittingly?)

---

[17] See especially Book V, §3-6.

uses concepts that go back to late antiquity and presents them in modern 'scientific' terminology ('ultimate observer' versus 'God'). It does not matter for the modern reader whether we take Dunne or Boethius as our point of departure. Flieger is able to explain Tolkien's concept of time without mentioning Boethius even once, and she must be credited with establishing Dunne's theories as an obvious influence on Tolkien – few people would have ever realised this if Flieger had not investigated the publications of the 1920s.[18] For this achievement I would like to express my admiration.

Yet as a mediaevalist I cannot but point out that Dunne is 'secondary', chronologically speaking as well as with regard to Tolkien, and that the primary inspiration is most likely from Boethius' *De Consolatione Philosophiae*. Unfortunately, I have not been able to check the handwritten notes in Tolkien's copy of Dunne's *An Experiment with Time*, but I can very well imagine that we would find a scribbled reference such as 'see Boethius V.6'.

CONCLUSION

Are mediaevalists 'better' readers of Tolkien? My very personal answer is a qualified 'yes'. Mediaevalists see more and are able to understand and use Tolkien's own standards in order to assess his work, whereas many literary critics are no longer even familiar with these standards, let alone being in sympathy with them.

---

[18] Alex Lewis and Elizabeth Curry, in their *The Uncharted Realms of Tolkien*, also aim at the exploration of the literary and cultural context of Tolkien's work

THOMAS HONEGGER holds a Ph.D. from the University of Zurich where he had been working as assistant and where he taught Old and Middle English. He is the author of *From Phoenix to Chauntecleer: Medieval English Animal Poetry* (1996) and has edited *News from the Shire and Beyond – Studies on Tolkien* (1997, together with Peter Buchs), *Root and Branch – Approaches towards Understanding Tolkien* (1999), *Authors, Heroes and Lovers* (2001), *Tolkien in Translation* (2003), *Translating Tolkien* (2004), and *Riddles, Knights, and Cross-Dressing Saints* (2004). Apart from his publications on animals and Tolkien, he has written about Chaucer, Shakespeare, and mediaeval romance. He is, since April 2002, Professor for Mediaeval Studies at the Friedrich-Schiller-University (Jena).
Homepage:
http://www2.uni-jena.de/fsu/anglistik/Struktur%20&%20Personal/Bereiche/Mediaevistik.html

References

AURNER, Nellie Slayton. *Hengest: A Study in Early English Hero Legend*. Iowa City: University of Iowa, 1921.

BEOWULF. (Edited by Fr. Klaeber; 3rd edition). Lexington, Massachusetts: D.C. Heath & Co.

BOETHIUS, Anicius Manlius Severinus. *De Consolatione Philosophiae*. (c. 523; translated by Victor Watts: *The Consolation of Philosophy*). London: Penguin, 1999.

BURNLEY, J. David. "Style, Meaning and Communication in *Sir Gawain and the Green Knight*". *Poetica* (Tokyo) 42 (1995): 23-37.

CARPENTER, Humphrey. *J.R.R. Tolkien: A Biography*. London: Unwin Hyman, 1977.

CARPENTER, Humphrey (edited with the assistance of C. Tolkien). *The Letters of J.R.R. Tolkien*. (First published 1981). Boston and New York: Houghton Mifflin, 2000.

CHANCE, Jane. *Tolkien's Art: A Mythology for England*. (First published 1979). Lexington: University Press of Kentucky. Revised edition, 2001.

DAMICO, Helen. *Beowulf's Wealhtheow and the Valkyrie Tradition*. Madison, Wisconsin: The University of Wisconsin Press, 1984.

DROUT, Michael. *Beowulf and the Critics by J.R.R. Tolkien*. (Medieval and Renaissance Texts and Studies Volume 248). Tempe, Arizona: Arizona Center for Medieval and Renaissance Studies, 2002.

DUNNE, J.W. *An Experiment with Time*. (First published 1927). Charlottesville, VA: Hampton Roads Publishing. Revised and enlarged edition, 2001.

ECCLES, Mark (ed.). *The Macro Plays: The Castle of Perseverance, Wisdom, Mankind*. (EETS OS 262). London and Oxford: Oxford University Press, 1969.

FLIEGER, Verlyn. *A Question of Time: J.R.R. Tolkien's Road to Faërie*. Kent, Ohio: The Kent State University Press, 1997.

GROTTA-KURSKA, Daniel. *J.R.R. Tolkien: Architect of Middle-earth*. Philadelphia: Running Press, 1976.

HARRISON, Mark. *Anglo-Saxon Thegn (AD 449-1066)*. Oxford: Osprey, 1993.

HONEGGER, Thomas. "Éowyn, Aragorn and the Hidden Dangers of Drink". *Inklings* 17 (1999): 217-225.

LAYAMON. *Brut*. (Edited by G.L. Brook and R.F. Leslie. EETS OS 250). London: Oxford University Press, 1963.

LEWIS, Alex and Elizabeth Currie. *The Uncharted Realms of Tolkien*. Oswestry: Medea Publishing, 2002.

RATELIFF, John. "Grima the Wormtongue: Tolkien and His Sources". *Mallorn* 25 (1988):15-17.

ROSEBURY, Brian. *Tolkien: A Cultural Phenomenon*. (First published 1992). Houndmills: Palgrave Macmillan. Revised and enlarged edition, 2003.

SHIPPEY, Tom A. *J.R.R. Tolkien: Author of the Century*. London: HarperCollins, 2000.

SHIPPEY, Tom A. *The Road to Middle-earth*. (First published 1982; 2nd edition 1992; 3rd edition 2003). New York: Houghton Mifflin, 2003.

SMITH, Mark Eddy. *Tolkien's Ordinary Virtues*. Downers Grove, Illinois: InterVarsity Press, 2002.

TOLKIEN, J.R.R. *The Lord of the Rings*. (First published 1954-55; second edition 1966). London: HarperCollins. One volume edition, 1992.

TOLKIEN, J.R.R. *The Treason of Isengard*. (Edited by C. Tolkien. History of Middle-earth volume 7). London: Unwin Hyman, 1989.

WEST, John G. Jr. (ed.). *Celebrating Middle-earth: The Lord of the Rings as a Defense of Western Civilisation*. Seattle: Inkling Books, 2002.

Thoughts on J.R.R. Tolkien's *The Lord of the Rings* and History

PAUL E. KERRY

Abstract

The Lord of the Rings is a work of fiction. Yet, Tolkien said that he "wanted people simply to get inside this story and take it (in as sense) as actual history". This essay examines what strategies are active in *The Lord of the Rings* that buttress the author's intention (and indeed the claims of the narrative itself) that it is a work of history. I start from the premise that philology in Tolkien's day was understood to be the fountainhead of cultural history. *The Lord of the Rings* invokes the Classical standard of an eyewitness, and the prologue and appendices strengthen the historical posture of the book by mimicking modern historical practices. *The Lord of the Rings* also blends Romantic and Enlightenment modes of historical writing. Finally, the book can be understood as a symbolic history and a genre of textual memory.

INTRODUCTION

Harold Bloom, the eminent American literary critic at Yale University, made one of the most enigmatic and yet strangely compelling comparisons when he likened Tolkien's *The Lord of the Rings* to *The Book of Mormon*, which along with the Bible occupies a central place in the scriptural canon of The Church of Jesus Christ of Latter-day Saints: "Sometimes, reading Tolkien, I am reminded of the Book of Mormon" (Bloom 1992:2). Bloom's lack of 'aesthetic' enthusiasm for both the Oxford don's literary masterpiece and the Vermont farm boy and later prophet Joseph Smith's translation of an ancient record is amplified when he writes that they suffer stylistically from a "heavy King James Bible influence" (Bloom 1992:2). But when once the comparison is made, a symmetry becomes apparent: both works are epic-like in scope,[1] dilate on the nature of good and evil, locate moral agency at the centre of the human condition, and prophesy the revelation of a long foretold King, Aragorn and the Lord Jesus Christ respectively. They are religious, following especially recent Catholic critics who argue that underlying *The Lord of the Rings* is "Catholic Christianity, the 'True Myth'" (Pearce 1999:84).[2] And both claim to be, to some degree, concerned with history.

The title page to *The Book of Mormon* reads:

> The Book of Mormon, an account written by the hand of Mormon upon plates taken from the plates of Nephi. Wherefore, it is an abridgment of the record of the people of Nephi, and also of the Lamanites [...] An abridgment taken from the Book of Ether also, which is a record of the people of Jared, who were scattered at the time the Lord confounded the language of the people.

Tolkien pronounced his historical intention openly in writing *The Lord of the Rings*: "I wanted people simply to get inside this story and take it (in a sense) as actual history" (Carpenter 1977:198-99). Jane Chance, following Humphrey Carpenter, sees Tolkien wanting to be a "discoverer of legend" (Chance 2001:2) and this is the guise he dons in *The Lord of the Rings*: a latter-day scholar who has come across ancient records

---

[1] Richard Dilworth Rust, Professor of English at the University of North Carolina, Chapel Hill, has shown in his study *Feasting on the Word: The Literary Testimony of the Book of Mormon* how *The Book of Mormon* meets the criteria for an epic. Professor Bloom has written on *The Book of Mormon* in *The American Religion: the Emergence of the Post-Christian Nation*.

[2] There has been a recent flurry of interpretations of the *The Lord of the Rings* from the Catholic perspective. Cf. Owen Dudley Edwards's "Gollum, Frodo and the Catholic Novel", Stratford Caldecott's *Secret Fire. The Spiritual Vision of J .R. R. Tolkien,* and Paul E. Kerry's "The Idea of Influence, J.R.R. Tolkien's *The Lord of the Rings*, and Catholicism: a Historian's Perspective".

and who is at pains to make them accessible to a modern audience. The point of this article is to show the strategies that Tolkien deploys to structure *The Lord of the Rings* in such a way so that it can be taken "(in a sense) as actual history."

PHILOLOGY

It is important to observe, at the outset, that Tolkien was first and foremost a philologist, a scholar of the nature and history of languages: "I am a philologist and all my work is philological" (as quoted in Birzer 2002:24). Tolkien's training in philology took place in the years when German scholarship dominated the discipline.[3] For in Germany, particularly as the discipline was formed in the nineteenth century, philology did not have the narrower linguistic meanings that some would associate with it today. *Philologie* was an all-encompassing discipline; it was the primary means of studying the linguistic elements of a language and also the key to understanding the culture of those who spoke the language.[4] In other words, it is crucial to keep in mind that philology was believed to be the fountainhead of cultural history: "Die Aufgabe der Philologie ist, jenes vergangene Leben durch die Kraft der Wissenschaft wieder le-

---

[3] Cf. Henry Cecil Kennedy Wyld's *English Philology in English Universities: an Inaugural Lecture Delivered in the Examination Schools on February 2, 1921*. Professor Wyld cites the moribund state of English philology, particularly in the areas of Middle and Old English, and writes that English monographs on those subjects reflect the "views and methods of the German philologists" and are often produced under the "influence of German Professors" (Wyld 1921:12-13). He later expresses his exasperation: "Are we at English Universities going to do these and many other things ourselves, or shall we leave them all for the foreigner?" (Wyld 1921:41). Cf. developments in the periodical *English and Germanic Studies* published from 1947-1961.

[4] Ransom, the hero of C. S. Lewis's trilogy, *Out of the Silent Planet*, *Perelandra*, and *That Hideous Strength*, is a philologist, who appears to have been modeled on his friend Tolkien. In *Out of the Silent Planet* Lewis shows how Ransom's philological skills gave him the ability to understand the different cultures he encountered. The philological aspect of Tolkien's writing is illuminated by Thomas A. Shippey without becoming overbearing in *J.R.R. Tolkien: Author of the Century*.

bendig zu machen" [The puprose of philology is to revive that past life [he refers to the Greco-Roman] through the power of science" (Wilamowitz-Moellendorff 1921:1). When attempting to understand Tolkien's moves as a historian it is crucial to keep this in mind, for as Thomas Honegger (2005:50) has observed, "many literary critics are no longer even familiar with [Tolkien's standards of medievalism and I would add philology], let alone being in sympathy with them."

The various languages in *The Lord of the Rings* are not an 'extra' which Tolkien added to make his work appear erudite; rather, they are essential elements in creating any kind of verisimilitude of Tolkien's cultures to actual histories. Of course, the languages represent much more than this in *The Lord of the Rings*, including the notion that language itself functioned in a world in which words contained a primeval power; nevertheless, for our purposes the creation of the languages is fundamental to the creation of the various peoples of Middle-earth that then and only then are capable of having their own history.

EYEWITNESSES

It is, therefore, no coincidence that Bilbo and Frodo are both writing a history of what has transpired in the discovery and destruction of the Ring. The act of creating a written record makes history possible in the first place, at least in the Classical sense. Herodotus and Thucydides are immensely different in their approach to history in *The Histories* and *The History of the Peloponnesian Wars*, respectively. They share, however, a similar methodology, for both historians claim to have been eye witnesses to the events that they describe. Bilbo and Frodo witnessed and participated in events that they then record. The tradition of a witness, which played an indispensable role in not only western religious and legal culture, but also in business culture (for example the early modern guilds), held sway for historians until Lord Clarendon's *The History of the Rebellion and Civil Wars in England*, published at the beginning of the eighteenth century. Thereafter it became more common for historians to use primary source documents (that is the writings of those who were a part of the history being narrated) about events that the historians had not themselves witnessed.

The Prologue to *The Lord of the Rings*, specifically the "Note on the Shire Records," provides a description of the process of transmission of the ancient records from Bilbo's original diaries, to Frodo's additions, culminating in the Red Book, of which many copies, of differing quality, were made over time (the original being lost). There is also an explanation that gives further evidence of scholarship and historicity: "Since Meriadoc and Peregrin became heads of their great families, and at the same time kept up their connexions with Rohan and Gondor, the libraries at Bucklebury and Tuckborough contained much that did not appear in the Red Book" (*LotR* 14).[5]

THE APPENDIX

The sense of history in *The Lord of the Rings* is not evenly distributed. Richard Jeffrey argues that the narrative becomes more historical as it progresses:

> [...] Book One, Frodo's journey as far as Rivendell with the other three hobbits and then with Strider, is the heart of the book; it is the only part which is practically as good as Tolkien the perfectionist could get it [...] [T]he whole has a unique compound of the qualities of a fairy-story and a myth, which gives an extraordinary power, and a sense of the strangeness and importance of the world, of familiar things, of

---

5 Similarly, to keep with Bloom's comparison, *The Book of Mormon* was "written by many ancient prophets by the spirit of prophecy and revelation. Their words, written on gold plates, were quoted and abridged by a prophet-historian named Mormon" (*Book of Mormon*, Introduction).

> ordinary decisions; a sense that our lives correspond deeply to this 'world being after all full of strange creatures beyond count', where a journey in any direction is likely to lead across huge tracts of empty wilderness to some quite unprecedented form of danger, or kindness, or beauty; [...] To me it's this book which casts a spell over all the rest of *The Lord of the Rings* and keeps the whole complexity alive. Much of the next volume and a half is almost as compelling (more in the character of myth and history, with less of the immediacy of fairy-story). (Jeffrey 1999:151)

The most overt structural attempt to engineer the historical veracity of *The Lord of the Rings* is the inclusion of the Appendix, actually several appendices. Paul Kocher summarises the salient points:

> This accolade of history and historical records [Tolkien] bestows frequently in both Prologue and Appendices. With the Shire Calendar in the year 1601 of the Third Age, states the Prologue, '... legend among the Hobbits first becomes history with a reckoning of years.' A few pages farther on, Bilbo's 111th birthday is said to have occurred in the Shire year 1401: 'At this point this History begins.'
> (Kocher 1972:3)

Appendix A, "Annals of the Kings and Rulers", draws on a medieval European technique to provide a compact political history and deep back story for *The Lord of the Rings* (*LotR* 1009); Appendix B is a chronology, another medieval historical device, with commentary that has as its focal point "The Great Years" of the Third Age (*LotR* 1065), which is the main narrative of *The Lord of the Rings*, but this appendix serves to give the immediate prehistory, as well as show how the War of the Ring is but a small (yet momentous) part of the overall history of

Middle-earth. Tolkien's appendices provide an important historical context for *The Lord of the Rings* and allowed him great creative scope:

> The historical information [...] tells us that we are coming into the story, not at the beginning, but rather near the end. That is, except for Chapter 1, we have a three-year view of a history which is demonstrably almost 7,000 years long, and uncountable years longer than that. [...] Tolkien can create an effect of great depth by reference and allusion. Middle-earth is rich in history because most of it has already taken place. Every locale seems to be a place where not only something is happening, but where something (or several things) happened long ago. (Stanton 2001:15)

Appendix C is a basic genealogy of some of the guests at Bilbo's "Farewell Party," which situates the family histories of key characters (*LotR* 1073); Appendix D demonstrates how the Shire calendar is to be used (*LotR* 1079); Appendix E relates to the conventions of spelling and writing in the Third Age and contains an excellent example of Tolkien's attempt to blur the boundaries between history and fiction. It features a rare and effective use of the first person, not dissimilar to the historical novelist Sir Walter Scott's framing devices in *Rob Roy* or his other historical novels:

> The Westron or Common Speech has been entirely translated into English equivalents [...] In transcribing the ancient scripts I have tried to represent the original sounds (so far as they can be determined) with fair accuracy, and at the same time to produce words and names that do not look uncouth in modern letters. (*LotR* 1087)

Appendix F introduces "The languages and the peoples of the Third Age" (*LotR* 1101). This critical apparatus goes well beyond relying on the reader's willing suspension of disbelief; it attempts to create in the language and organizing principles of traditional scholarship a sense of reality – a sense of history – for Tolkien's subcreated world.[6] The reader's imagination uses the nearly tangible ruins provided in the appendices to build up the world of Middle-earth.

Tolkien's appendices do not break with the narrative; they deepen and extend it by sketching genealogies, providing alphabets, giving dates, inserting key historical data, etc. One could also argue that Tolkien's appendices are a continuation of the narrative (indeed, *The Lord of the Rings* becomes at once richer and yet diminutive when placed in its context), and all of this before Hollywood knew too much about sequels and prequels. Tolkien is careful to remain a scholar in the Appendix and this reinforces the notion that *The Lord of the Rings* is history, for its tone and presentation mimic the prevailing practices of the historical profession.

HISTORY, LITERATURE, AND NARRATIVE

The Lord of the Rings can be understood as history if one concedes that historical novelists such as Tolstoy, Scott, or George Eliot produce history by other means, by interweaving history and literature, scholarship and imagination. If so, then Tolkien can be seen to do something similar. Of course, historical novelists base their narratives around actual socio-political events, and their novels are powerful historical interpretations of those events. Tolkien's work is very different in this regard in

---

[6] It is interesting to note that modern novels, such as Dan Brown's *The Da Vinci Code* (2003), try to create a similar sense of reality with indications of archival research, links to websites, companion volumes, etc.

that he invented the entire history, even the cosmogony, of Middle-earth.[7]

Since this essay started with a unique comparison, let me make another. The structuring device of the appendices, though not necessarily its function reminds me of the epilogues that Tolstoy places at the end of *War and Peace*. Isaiah Berlin was not the first to notice the profound insights that Tolstoy makes in this lengthy addendum, but he recognized that here was an entire approach to history (Berlin *passim*). For Tolstoy, unlike Tolkien, philosophizes on the nature of history and at the point of the epilogues the reader can look back on *War and Peace* as an example of exquisite historical practice in addition to the myriad other things that the work embodies.

Tolstoy presents us with historical reasoning; Tolkien with the stuff of history. The intellectual historian, Collingwood, suggested that all attempts at history are a kind of re-enactment, and this lens sheds light on why Tolkien enthusiasts can find ways to recreate Middle-earth in everything from language to costume, for Tolkien's vividness and detail allow readers to enter into what appears to be a historical world. Brian Rosebury argues that "the temporal and spatial order, the historico-geographical extension and density [...] are attributes of the real universe" and therefore *The Lord of the Rings* is "unusually mimetic" because it displays psychological and physical realism and contains "historical correlatives" (Rosebury 2003:15-20).

For Tolkien, as for the narrative historians of the nineteenth century from at least Friedrich Schiller to Jules Michelet, Thomas Macaulay, and Thomas Carlyle, narrative is the means of expressing

---

[7] Professor Edward James, a medieval historian at the University of Reading, pointed out to me that medieval cosmologies could be viewed as the science fiction or fantasy writing of their day. To some degree the appendices to *The Lord of the Rings*, but more especially Tolkien's *The Silmarillion*, present a cosmogony, a description of the origin of the world.

history. Tolkien's historical approach reminds me in some ways of Carlyle. Carlyle is typically associated with his successful history, *The French Revolution* (1837). In this work, as in his *Oliver Cromwell* (1845), the reader enters into the vivid historical paintings that Carlyle creates to take part in his history, because for Carlyle history is dead unless it is relived. The apparatus of the appendices and prologue of *The Lord of the Rings* provide much more than a historical frame, but they are not the history, as tempting and easy as it is to classify them as such and then have done with it. The narrative of the book is itself the history that is to be lived.

Patrick Curry makes a fresh comparison along the lines of Tolkien's narrative technique, by juxtaposing it to those ruminated on by Walter Benjamin in "The Storyteller" and he concludes that for Tolkien "narrative fantasy" is "'a recognition of fact, but not a slavery to it'" (Curry 1997:141).[8] Orson Scott Card expounds:

> Tolkien does not want you to read his stories, decoding as you go. He wants you to immerse yourself in the tale, and care about what the characters do and why they do it. He wants you to feel frustrated when the Steward tries to burn his son alive, and relieved when his son's life is saved. He does not want you to start wondering if this is some sort of undoing of the Christ myth, or perhaps an allusion to the Akedah, in which the father offers his son as sacrifice only to have the sacrifice stopped at the last minute, with the father himself serving as "ram in the thicket." He does not want you to think of how this is really an analogy to the way the authority-loving patriarchy destroys its male children. (Card 2001:156)

---

8   Cf. David K. Miller's "Narrative Pattern in *The Fellowship of the Ring*".

The historian Hayden White has argued in several places that history, particularly its modes of narrative construction, is another genre of fiction.[9] Tolkien attempts to show this from the other side, to make a fictional narrative historical. Bradley Birzer detected precisely this point from within the narrative itself: "Little difference, Tolkien's characters state, exists between history and myth, or between the historian and the minstrel. Indeed, the minstrel may understand the complexities of life far more than the historian, trapped in his archives and specialized, cramped world" (Birzer 2001:25). Rendel Helms has pointed out that the cause-and-effect sequences which form the basis for literary realism are the same for the fantasy genre:

> Fantasy stands upon a different theory of reality, but one demanding with equal rigor that the fantasist keep always in mind his aesthetic principles: that what happens in his world accord not with his daydreams nor with our own world's laws of common sense, but with the peculiar laws of the sub-created cosmos. (Helms 1974:77)

Once the reader submits to this tacit condition and accepts that the "interior authenticity" achieved by "a resourceful deployment of what can only be called realistic elements" (Rosebury 2003:19), then the fantasy world becomes credible, perhaps not unlike the way that J. K. Rowling's *Harry Potter* series or Philip Pullman's *His Dark Materials* trilogy work.

HISTORY AS APPLICABILITY

The Romantic mode of Michelet or Carlyle is far away from certain Enlightenment views, for example those of Bolingbroke or Voltaire,

---

[9] See especially *Metahistory: The Historical Imagination in Nineteenth-Century Europe*.

who used history to throw the present into relief by showing how similar moral laws operated from one generation to another or who used the past didactically, to change the present. And it is precisely in this way that some read *The Lord of the Rings*. For example, the "Scouring of the Shire" can be seen as a veiled social criticism springing from the destruction of the English countryside during the postwar era. In 1966 Tolkien attempted to nip this kind of criticism in the bud: "it has been supposed by some that 'The Scouring of the Shire' reflects the situation in England at the time when I was finishing my tale. It does not." But he concedes: "It has indeed some basis in experience, though slender [...] and much further back. [...] The country in which I lived in childhood was being shabbily destroyed before I was ten, in days when motor-cars were rare objects (I had never seen one) and men were still building suburban railways" (*LotR* xvii). Regardless, *The Lord of the Rings* has been read as an allegory of the Great War (and indeed the events leading up to World War II and thereafter), an interpretation that is gaining popularity once again.[10] Tolkien famously spoke out against allegory in the 1966 "Foreword" to the second edition of *The Lord of the Rings*, but he did suggest that the concept of applicability, particularly in relation to history, was productive:

> I much prefer history, true or feigned, with its varied applicability to the thought and experience of readers. I think that many confuse 'applicability' with 'allegory'; but the one resides in the freedom of the reader, and the other in the purposed domination of the author. (*LotR* xvii)

---

[10] For a sampling of this line of inquiry, cf. Roger Sale's *Modern Heroism: Essays on D. H. Lawrence, William Empson, & J. R. R. Tolkien* (pp. 237-39), Thomas A. Shippey's *J.R.R. Tolkien: Author of the Century* (chapter four), Robert Plank's "'The Scouring of the Shire': Tolkien's View of Fascism", and John Garth's *Tolkien and the Great War: The Threshold of Middle-earth*.

This would fit with certain didactic strategies of the eighteenth century that used history to provide examples of universal standards and laws that applied to both past and present.

SYMBOLIC HISTORY

The Lord of the Rings has its creative roots in Tolkien's twentieth-century experience and although it does not describe these allegorically, one could argue that it creates from these events a symbolic history. W. H. Auden recognized something like this when he analyzed *The Lord of the Rings* as a Quest:

> The Quest is one of the oldest, hardiest, and most popular of all literary genres. In some instances it may be founded on historical fact – the Quest of the Golden Fleece may have its origins in the search of seafaring traders for amber – and certain themes, like the theme of the enchanted cruel Princess whose heart can be melted only by the predestined lover, may be distorted recollections of religious rites, but the persistent appeal of the Quest as literary form is due, I believe, to its validity as a symbolic description of our subjective personal experience of existence as historical. (Auden 1972:42)

Tolkien did not have actual historical events to draw on, so he invented them and embedded *The Lord of the Rings* within them. The philological consistency of the languages, as well as the carefully presented historical detail, could be perceived as an attempt to show that 'this actually happened,' alluding to the nineteenth-century German historian Leopold von Ranke, a figure commonly associated with modern historical methods. On the other hand, all that is needed for a symbolic history is for the reader to allow that 'this might have happened,' in the way that Arthurian legends appeal, and then the door is opened to an alternate or counter-factual historical mode. The eminent Oxford historian Hugh Trevor-Roper explains why this mode (often eschewed by professional historians) is a valuable way of conceiving history:

> For in the end, it is the imagination of the historian, not his scholarship or his method (necessary though these are), which will discern the hidden forces of change. This, I suppose, is what Theodor Mommsen meant when he spoke of the divinatory gift of the historian, and this is what Jacob Burckhardt meant when he spoke of *Ahnung*, contemplation, the capacity 'to see the present lying in the past'. [...] Such is the imagination of which historical writing, and historical study, will always, I think, have need. To exercise such imagination may not be within our power as historians; but to allow its importance, to recognise it when it is exercised, is, I believe, essential if we are to keep historical study among the humane subjects, to keep it alive.
> (Trevor-Roper 1981:368-69)

The Lord of the Rings is Tolkien's *Ahnung*, his idea of the presence of the past.

CONCLUSION

To return to Bloom, *The Lord of the Rings* might be compared to *The Book of Mormon* in another way: they provide access to a voice "speaking out of the dust."[11] I have argued that Tolkien invents the very primary sources needed for an actual history, but if one follows Thomas Honegger's argument, Middle-earth is laced with intertextual medieval

---

[11] Moroni 10:27. On the dust of history, see Carolyn Steedman's *Dust: the Archive of Cultural History*.

references and draws freely on medieval sources, an actual world within Tolkien's universe (Honegger 2005). Jane Chance has called this the "medievalization of [Tolkien's] mythology" (Chance 2001:ix). Fred West asserts that *The Lord of the Rings* is a "virtual resurrection of the literary forms and themes" of the "glorious melting pot of Greco-Roman, Judeo-Christian, and pagan North European cultures" (West 2002:16).

The ancient sources and references in and the medievalization of *The Lord of the Rings* are strategies to keep precisely those parts of European history *alive* (to use Trevor-Roper's formulation) to which Tolkien devoted all of his professional life and much of his personal energy. Perhaps Tolkien sensed what C. S. Lewis did in his 1954 inaugural lecture entitled "De Descriptione Temporum" at the University of Cambridge when Lewis became Professor of Medieval and Renaissance Literature and was a Fellow at Magdalene College. He told the students: "I read as a native texts that you must read as foreigners" and he referred to himself as one of the "Old Western men" (Lewis 1955:21). In his lecture he suggested that students would have an increasingly limited understanding of the actual ancient cultures that he had studied and in which he had found rich sources of knowledge and experience. On 9 November 2004 another Fellow of Magdalene College, Nicholas Boyle, Professor of German literary and intellectual history in the University of Cambridge, addressed the Fall Faculty Convocation at Georgetown University: "The human world is constituted by language and language is at its core a tradition, a handing on of signs and meanings, a medium through which the voices of all previous users reverberate" (Boyle 2004:11).

Considered in this way, *The Lord of the Rings* is an ingenious music box that when opened strikes chords that remind hearers of the ancient melodies that may yet be faintly heard in much of modernity. *The Lord of the Rings* is a genre of textual memory; a distillation of Tolkien's learning and moral vision that synthesizes and preserves what he valued in European cultural history.

PAUL E. KERRY is an intellectual historian whose training spans several universities including Chicago, Harvard, and Oxford where he completed his D.Phil. at St. John's College. He has been a visiting research fellow at the University of Reading (History) and the University of Edinburgh (IASH). In 2003-2004 he was invited to The Queen's College, Oxford and was a Senior Visiting Research Scholar in the Modern European History Research Centre. His publications have engaged with the history of ideas, historiography, interdisciplinary history, modern Jewish history, the Enlightenment, and Romanticism. He has published a book on *Enlightenment Thought in the Writings of Goethe* (2001), and edited books on *Goethe and Religion* (2000), *The Magic Flute* (2004), *Thomas Carlyle*, and *Friedrich Schiller* (forthcoming 2005). Dr Kerry was elected a Fellow of the Royal Historical Society in 2003. He is currently an Assistant Professor at Brigham Young University and a Visiting Fellow at the University of Cambridge in the Centre for Research in the Arts, Social Sciences and Humanities where he is completing a book on German intellectual history; he is also a Visiting Scholar in the Department of History and affiliated with Pembroke College. In 2006 he will be a Research Associate at the University of Pennsylvania's McNeil Center for Early American Studies.

References

AUDEN, W. H. 1972. "The Quest Hero" in *Tolkien and the Critics. Essays on J.R.R. Tolkien's The Lord of the Rings*, edited by Neil D. ISAACS and Rose A. ZIMBARDO. Notre Dame, Indiana: University of Notre Dame Press, 40-61.

BERLIN, Isaiah. 1993. *The Hedgehog and the Fox: An Essay on Tolstoy's View of History*. Chicago: Ivan R. Dee.

BIRZER, Bradley J. 2002. *J.R.R. Tolkien's Sanctifying Myth. Understanding Middle-earth*, with a foreword by Joseph PEARCE. Wilmington, Delaware: ISI Books.

BLOOM, Harold. 1992. *The American Religion: The Emergence of the Post-Christian Nation*. New York: Simon and Schuster.

BLOOM, Harold (ed.). 2000. *J.R.R. Tolkien's The Lord of the Rings. Modern Critical Interpretations*, edited and with an introduction by Harold BLOOM. Philadelphia: Chelsea House.

Book of Mormon. 1986 (originally published 1830). Salt Lake City, Utah: The Church of Jesus Christ of Latter-day Saints.

BOYLE, Nicholas. 2004. "Georgetown University Fall Faculty Convocation Address 9 November 2004". Unpublished MS, 1-14.

CALDECOTT, Stratford. 2003. *Secret Fire. The Spiritual Vision of J.R.R. Tolkien*. London: Darton, Longman, Todd.

CARD, Orson Scott. 2001. "How Tolkien Means" in *Meditations on Middle-Earth*, edited by Karen HABER. New York: St. Martin's Griffen, 153-174.

CARPENTER, Humphrey. 1977. *J.R.R. Tolkien: A Biography*. London: HarperCollins, 1995.

CHANCE, Jane. 2001. *Tolkien's Art. A Mythology for England*, revised edition, first edition 1979. Lexington, Kentucky: University Press of Kentucky.

COLLINGWOOD, R. G. 1994. *The Idea of History*, revised edition, edited and with an introduction by Jan VAN DER DUSSEN. Oxford: Oxford University Press.

CURRY, Patrick. 1997. *Defending Middle-Earth. Tolkien: Myth and Modernity*. London: HarperCollins, 1998.

EDWARDS, Owen Dudley, 2003. "Gollum, Frodo and the Catholic Novel" in *A Hidden Presence: The Catholic Imagination of J.R.R. Tolkien*, edited by Stratford CALDECOTT. South Orange, New Jersey: The Chesteron Press.

GARTH, John. 2003. *Tolkien and the Great War: The Threshold of Middle-earth*. London: HarperCollins.

HELMS, Rendel. 1974. *Tolkien's World*. Boston: Houghton Mifflin, 1974.

HONEGGER, Thomas, 2005. "Tolkien through the Eyes of a Mediaevalist" in *Reconsidering Tolkien*, edited by Thomas HONEGGER. Zurich and Berne: Walking Tree Publishers, 55-66.

JEFFREY, Richard. 1999. "Root and Tree: The Growth of Tolkien's Writings" in *Tolkien: A Celebration. Collected Writings on a Literary Legacy*, edited by Joseph PEARCE. London: Fount, 141-155.

KERRY, Paul E. "The Idea of Influence, J.R.R. Tolkien's *The Lord of the Rings* and Catholicism: a Historian's Perspective", unpublished MS forthcoming in the Peter Roe series of the Tolkien Society U.K.

KOCHER, Paul H. 1972. *Master of Middle-earth: The Fiction of J.R.R. Tolkien*. Boston: Houghton Mifflin.

LEWIS, C. S. 1955. *De Descriptione Temporum. An Inaugural Lecture*. Cambridge: Cambridge University Press.

MILLER, David K. 2003. "Narrative Pattern in *The Fellowship of the Ring*" in *A Tolkien Compass* (first edition 1975), edited by Jared LOBDELL. Peru, Illinois: Open Court, 93-104.

PEARCE, Joseph. 1999. *Tolkien: Man and Myth*. London: HarperCollins.

PLANK, Robert. 2003. "'The Scouring of the Shire': Tolkien's View of Fascism" in *A Tolkien Compass* (first edition 1975), edited by Jared LOBDELL. Peru, Illinois: Open Court, 105-114.

ROSEBURY, Brian. 2003. *Tolkien: A Cultural Phenomenon*. Houndsmills, Basingstoke: Palgrave Macmillan.

RUST, Richard Dilworth. 1997. *Feasting on the Word: The Literary Testimony of the Book of Mormon*. Salt Lake City, Utah: Deseret.

SALE, Roger. 1973. *Modern Heroism: essays on D. H. Lawrence, William Empson, & J.R.R. Tolkien*. Berkeley: University of California Press.

SHIPPEY, Thomas A. 2000. *J.R.R. Tolkien: Author of the Century*. London: HarperCollins.

STANTON, Michael N. 2001. *Hobbits, Elves, and Wizards. Exploring the Wonders and Worlds of J.R.R. Tolkien's The Lord of the Rings*. New York: Palgrave Macmillan.

STEEDMAN, Carolyn. 2002. *Dust: The Archive of Cultural History*. New Brunswick, New Jersey: Rutgers University Press.

TOLKIEN, J.R.R. 1954-55. *The Lord of the Rings*. London: HarperCollins. One volume edition 1995.

TREVOR-ROPER, H.R. 1981. "History and Imagination" in *History and Imagination. Essays in Honour of H. R. Trevor-Roper*, edited by Hugh LLOYD-JONES, Valerie PEARL, and Blair WORDEN. London: Duckworth, 356-69.

WEST, Fred. 2002. "*The Lord of the Rings* as a Defense of Western Civilization" in *Celebrating Middle-Earth. The Lord of the Rings as a Defense of Western Civilization*, edited by Fred WEST. Seattle, Washington: Inkling Books, 15-30.

WHITE, Hayden V. 1975. *Metahistory: The Historical Imagination in Nineteenth-Century Europe*. Baltimore: Johns Hopkins University Press.

WILAMOWITZ-MOELLENDORFF, Ulrich von. 1921. *Geschichte der Philologie*. Leipzig: Teubner.

WYLD, Henry Cecil Kennedy. 1921. *English Philology in English Universities: An Inaugural Lecture Delivered in the Examination Schools on February 2, 1921*. Oxford: Clarendon.

The Knife, the Sting and the Tooth: Manifestations of Shadow in *The Lord of the Rings*

NATASA TUCEV

Abstract

This paper will attempt an archetypal analysis of Tolkien's narrative in order to demonstrate the centrality of the motif of shadow, a mythological term adopted by Jung to refer to undesirable and suppressed aspects of both the personal and collective psyche. The paper focuses on Tolkien's treatment of this motif with a view to exposing cultural and anthropological implications of his work, as well as his concept of personal growth, as exemplified by his protagonist Frodo. It is demonstrated that the collective shadow contents of Tolkien's imaginary universe, which is predominantly patriarchal, originate in the projection of Thanatos and the hostility towards the daemonic, orgiastic (and hence disruptive) elements of the feminine. At the personal level, however, Tolkien is more hopeful and examines the prospect of integrating the shadow through the complex dynamic evolving between Frodo and Gollum as his Other. The process whereby this integration is achieved is gradual and the psychological experiences it entails – withdrawing projections, relinquishing the ideological constructs which justify animosity towards the Other, and recovering wholeness by recognizing the disowned portion of the Self – may all be discerned in Tolkien's novel.

INTRODUCTION

On the journey back home, after he has completed his heroic quest, Frodo suddenly realizes that he has saved his native Shire for others, but not for himself:

> 'There is no real going back. Though I may come to the Shire, it will not seem the same; for I shall not be the same. I am wounded with knife, sting and tooth,

and a long burden. Where shall I find rest?'
(*LotR* 1026)[1]

Frodo's conscious outlook has been irrevocably changed by the disturbing revelations of his experiences and, like Eliot's Magi, he can no longer feel at ease in the old dispensation. As a metaphor for his lost innocence and limited awareness about reality and the self prior to undertaking his inward and outward journey, the Shire can no longer contain Frodo, whose comprehension had to expand in order to acknowledge and encompass his encounters with the dark side of the psyche.

The central place in Tolkien's narrative is assigned to Frodo and three other hobbits, whom the other races of Middle-Earth also call "halflings". The notion of a "halfling" is indicative of Tolkien's purpose to exploit his characters' potential for growth and transformation. In the course of their journey, each of the half-formed little men will symbolically grow up in a different way. Merry and Pippin will embrace the patriarchal order governing the race of Men, entering the armed services of human kingdoms and swearing oaths of fealty to the powerful father-figures of Théoden and Denethor (as Merry says to Théoden quite explicitly: "As a father you shall be to me" [*LotR* 809]).[2] Sam, a gardener, will be initiated in quite a different way, by receiving a box of earth and a magical *mallorn* seed from the sorceress of Lothlórien, the Elven-queen Galadriel. His affiliation with the feminine principle becomes especially prominent towards the end of the novel, when he uses Galadriel's gift to restore vegetative life in the Shire, and fathers a beautiful daughter Elanor.[3] Frodo's own journey towards self-realization is

---

[1] All quotations from *The Lord of the Rings* (*LotR*) are from the one-volume paperback edition (Tolkien 1995).

[2] In order to make their maturing more rounded and comprehensive, however, Tolkien will also arrange their crucial encounter with the ancient tree-shepherd Fangorn, whose draught makes Merry and Pippin grow three inches each.

[3] At the same time, however, he is bound to his beloved master Frodo, and symbolically 'split' between the two services. Steven Walker (2002:157) discusses the

the most complex of all, most far-reaching but at the same time the most troublesome, as it involves recognition and – at least to some degree – assimilation of the shadow.

Shadow, according to Jung, is a mythological name for an archetype which has the most frequent and the most disturbing influence on the ego. In so far as its nature is personal, it can be defined as the dark side of the ego-complex, the counterpart of the ego, created by the conscious mind and containing suppressed and undesirable aspects of personality. The shadow may also contain childish or primitive qualities which have a potential to vitalize and embellish human existence, provided they can be properly reintegrated. It is the most accessible of the archetypes, and the easiest to experience. On the other hand, since gaining shadow awareness (i.e., recognizing the negative traits of one's own personality) requires a considerable moral effort, it very often meets with resistance. Jung himself criticized fiercely the "foolish Jungians" who avoid the shadow and focus on other archetypes. For him, to indulge in the exploration of the more fascinating but less disturbing areas of the unconscious while sidestepping the distasteful problem of the shadow is equivalent to resisting self-knowledge. There can be no proper self-knowledge without the essential recognition of the presence and reality of one's shadowy side (Walker 2002:34-35).

The shadow also has its transpersonal dimension; as Steven Walker writes:

---

same-gender pairs of characters in myth and literature, such as Gilgamesh and Enkidu, Jim and Huck, Frodo and Sam, and refers to the archetype presiding over their relationships as the archetype of *the double*. It covers a number of psychological relations "based on feelings of affinity and identity [...] including [although not necessarily] passionate sexual attachment to a person of the same sex." There is certainly a potential for personal growth in such bonds, just as there is in heterosexual ones, guided by the archetype of Jungian *hieros gamos*.

> The *collective shadow*, viewed as a component of the collective unconscious, is the archetype of collective evil and can be represented by such archetypal images as the Devil, the Enemy, the Bad Guys, and the Evil Empire. In wartime or in any other situation of political confrontation the shadow is likely to be *projected* onto the enemy side, which is consequently viewed as hopelessly depraved, vicious, cruel, and inhuman [...] At the same time our side, having projected its shadow contents onto the enemy, appears to be all good and thoroughly justified [...] The myth of combat between Good and Evil often covers up a situation of moral unconsciousness, with inflation with the Good and projection of Evil [as] the usual result. (Walker 2002:34)

Apparently, there must be a causal relationship between the collective shadow of a given culture and the personal shadow: C. Zweig and S. Wolf, the authors of *Romancing the Shadow*, point out that the collective shadow "forms the sea of moral and social values in which we swim"; it provides a general framework whereby an individual establishes which traits of his/her character would be considered desirable or undesirable by the community, and in this way inevitably plays a part in constituting one's personal shadow (Zweig and Wolf 1997:17).

The shadow which Frodo encounters on his quest also consists of multiple layers, some of them referring to the cultural and anthropological dimensions of Tolkien's work, and some to how he conceived of the personal growth of his hero. Perhaps the best way to distinguish between them is to analyse the significance of the three wounds Frodo receives, and of the shadow figures inflicting them.

THE KNIFE

On Weathertop, Frodo is stabbed by a Morgul-knife, the weapon wielded by the Witch-king, the leader and the most terrifying of the nine Ringwraiths. While the others see the wraiths only as vague black shapes, Frodo gets a clearer view of them once he puts on the Ring. Symbolically, when one wears the Ring, the visible portion of the self – the *persona* one normally presents to the world – becomes invisible; whereas to the bearer, the concealed, suppressed portions of inner and outer reality become visible. The Ring acts as a catalyst, enabling one to encounter the shadow. This is why Galadriel refers to Frodo as "the one that has borne it [the Ring] on his finger and seen that which is hidden" (*LotR* 385).

The Ringwraiths were originally mortal men, "proud and great". "Long ago they fell under the dominion of the One, and they became shadows under his [the Dark Lord Sauron's] great Shadow, his most terrible servants" (*LotR* 65). Primarily, the Ringwraiths are the embodiment of the collective shadow of the race of Men. The story of the dreams and aspirations of the god-like human race of Númenoreans, and of their gradual decay, is told in fragments throughout the novel. A part of it is rehearsed by Faramir, the younger son of the steward of Gondor. Faramir discloses to Frodo and Sam his vision of the ideal of human civilization epitomized in a beautiful city treasuring ancient lore and historical records, wherein weapons are only to be used to defend its virtues:

> War must be, while we defend our lives against a destroyer who would devour all; but I do not love the bright sword for its sharpness, nor the arrow for its swiftness, nor the warrior for his glory. I love only that which they defend: the city of the Men of Númenor; and I would have her loved for her memory, her ancientry, her beauty, and her present wisdom. (*LotR* 698)

Most of the other inhabitants of Gondor, however, are unlike Faramir. (In terms of William James, Faramir might be denoted as one of the minority of "tender-minded" living in a "tough-minded" culture, of which his brother Boromir and his father Denethor would be typical representatives.[4]) He regretfully observes the slow regression of Númenoreans, from a race originally nearly divine in their virtues, wisdom and longevity, to a race of "Middle Men", "Men of the Twilight": "[...] we now love war and valour as things good in themselves, both a sport and an end; [...] we esteem a warrior [...] above men of other crafts" (*LotR* 705)

In Faramir's speech, the regressive indulgence of Númenoreans in war games and violence is in some vague way related to their obsession with death and the transience of human existence:

> Death was ever present, because the Númenoreans still [...] hungered after endless life unchanging. Kings made tombs more splendid than houses of the living, and counted old names in the rolls of their descent dearer than the names of sons. Childless lords sat in

---

[4] James maintains that within every culture there exist two types of personalities: the *tough-minded*, forming the majority, who by temperament are satisfied with normative culture and do not need to seek reality beyond its confines; and the *tender-minded*, the minority who feel alienated from the usual goals of their culture and are therefore led to explore beyond the ordinary. For this explanation of James's views I am indebted to Curtiss Hoffman's study *The Seven Story Tower* (1999:70).

aged halls musing on heraldry; in secret chambers withered men compounded strong elixirs, or in high cold towers asked questions of the stars. (*LotR* 704)

In effect, the patriarchal civilization of Númenor is obsessed by the need to defeat mortality and triumph over Nature. The Númenoreans become warriors, projecting Thanatos upon the Other. "Hungering after endless life unchanging", they refuse to accept death as a natural and inevitable phase of the biological cycle of human life. As a consequence, what inadvertently gets exiled into the shadow, alongside with their fear of death, is their vitality, as the images of childless lords and withered men suggest. What emerges from the shadow are nine bestial wraiths, mirroring mankind's own hidden face of destructiveness and dark obsession with power over life and death. The Witch-king of the Nazgûl becomes quite explicitly the personification of Thanatos, saying to Gandalf: "Old fool! This is my hour. Do you not know Death when you see it?" (*LotR* 861) In the scene of the battle of Minas Tirith, the entire dark host of Mordor, of deformed mindless creatures, orcs and trolls, embodying the suppressed and consequently demonized forces of Nature, is depicted ramming the gate of the beautiful white city of the seven circles, threatening to overwhelm the fragile ordered world of narrow human consciousness.

The account of the decay of Númenoreans also acquires a mythological dimension in its relation to the history of the Ring. In the novel's ancient pre-history Isildur, king Elendil's son, wastes his chance to throw the Ring into the fires of Mount Doom and thus to dispose of its evil forever, deciding instead to keep it in his possession, as an heirloom of his house and his descendants. Soon after this decision, Isildur is slain; the Ring becomes consequently known as *Isildur's Bane*, and we are told that "ever since that day the race of Númenor has decayed, and the span of their years has lessened" (*LotR* 261). The soft spot of Isildur, the most distinguished representative of Númenoreans, is by implication the soft spot of his whole culture. The accursed heritage which his heir Aragorn has to claim after years of self-imposed exile concerns not only the throne of Gondor, but also the recognition of the shadow of his race, epitomized in Isildur's tragic failure: the capacity for evil and betrayal of the noblest cultural ideals. When Aragorn expresses his conviction that "Isildur's heir should labour to repair Isildur's fault" (*LotR* 269), this entails far more than just wielding the sword.

THE STING

In order to enter Mordor, the realm of Sauron, and so commence the final phase of his quest, Frodo must follow his treacherous dark double, Gollum, into the dark tunnel which is really the lair of a gigantic she-spider Shelob. Mating with and later slaying her own male offspring, feeding on all living things, Shelob is depicted as an insatiable and thoroughly destructive female monster:

> Great horns she had, and behind her short stalk-like neck was her huge swollen body, a vast bloated bag, swaying and sagging between her legs; its great bulk was black, blotched with livid marks, but the belly underneath was pale and luminous and gave forth a stench. (*LotR* 752)
>
> [...] still she was there, who was there before Sauron [...] and she served none but herself, drinking the blood of Elves and Men, bloated and grown fat with endless brooding on her feasts, weaving webs of shadow; for all living things were her food, and her vomit darkness. Far and wide her lesser broods, bastards of the miserable mates, her own offspring, that she slew, spread from glen to glen [...](*LotR* 750)
>
> Little she knew of or cared for towers, or rings, or anything devised by mind or hand, who only desired death for all others, mind and body, and for her-

self a glut of life, alone, swollen till the mountains could no longer hold her up and the darkness contain her. (*LotR* 751)

The above is possibly one of the most striking literary representations of Jungian Terrible Mother, whom Ted Hughes also calls the Black Witch or the Queen of Hell. As Hughes explains, the Great Goddess of matriarchal mysteries consists of two antithetical figures – the Goddess of Benign Love and the Goddess of the Underworld (although the benign figure is sometimes further divided into Mother and Sacred Bride). In the most ancient manifestations, such as in Tiamat, the two are united, whereas in pairs such as Aphrodite and Persephone, or Inanna and Ereshkigal, the separation becomes more prominent. Still, as Hughes maintains, in every epiphany of the Goddess both aspects are present, "one latent behind the other. In the foreground they appear to be two, and opposites, but in the background they are one" (Hughes 1993:6-7). The rational ego of the patriarchal man, however, finds it impossible to cope with the Goddess in her completeness (even though, on the inner plane, she actually represents the totality of his natural, biological and instinctual life). In order to preserve the equilibrium and control required of him by society, he splits the Goddess into the part that supports and confirms his rational existence, and the part that would disrupt it. The dark, rejected part

> [...] not only includes the orgiastic, amoral and even non-human biological drive for reproduction [...] but associates herself, being forbidden, with everything forbidden, uncontrollable, naturally or supernaturally hostile, thereby uniting the world of death with the

world of elemental sexuality, animality and the daemonic (Hughes 1993:513-515).[5]

Frodo's encounter with Shelob is not fatal: "her Ladyship", as the orcs call her, stings him but does not kill him. He does, however, slip into a death-like state and Sam later finds him naked in the tower of Cirith Ungol. The symbolical death and rebirth perhaps constitute a prerequisite for entering "the land of Mordor where the Shadows lie."

The Elven-queen Galadriel (whose other titles include "The White Lady", "Lady that Dies Not" and "Mistress of Magic") represents the Goddess in her benign aspect. The following excerpt from Robert Graves's study leaves hardly any doubt that Galadriel and Shelob are split manifestations of the same archetype:

> The Goddess is a lovely, slender woman with [...] deathly pale face, lips red as rowan-berries, startlingly blue eyes and long fair hair; she will suddenly transform herself into sow, mare, bitch, vixen, she-ass, weasel, serpent, owl, she-wolf, tigress, mermaid or loathsome hag. [...] In ghost stories she often figures as "The White Lady", and in ancient religions, from the British Isles to Caucasus, as the "White Goddess" [...]. [A] true poem is necessarily an invocation of the White Goddess, or Muse, the mother of All Living, the ancient power of fright and lust – the female spider or the queen-bee whose embrace is death. (Graves 1961:24)

---

[5] Ted Hughes also notices that "the imagination's symbols are based on subliminal perception." According to him, Shakespeare's close acquaintance with farm life significantly contributed to the hold that the myth of Venus and Adonis had on his imagination, and to his choice of boar/sow as a symbol of "elemental sexuality and animality." Similarly, the fact that Tolkien was stung by a spider in childhood must have made a corresponding impact on his mythic equation.

Quoting Shakespeare and a fourteenth-century charm, Graves gives evidence for yet another mythical manifestation of the Goddess, in the form of the cruel Night Mare. In these epiphanies Night Mare is accompanied by offspring: St Swithold in Shakespeare's verses encounters "the Night Mare and her nine-fold", the nine young ones who "suck up blood" just like their mother (Graves 1961:26). Given that in the first part of Tolkien's novel the nine Ringwraiths appear in the form of Black Riders, it is possible that by their mythological background they are also related to the rejected half of the feminine. They certainly do belong to the same complex of unconscious fears of everything "forbidden, uncontrollable, naturally or supernaturally hostile", "the world of death and the daemonic" with which Hughes associates the insatiable and amoral Queen of Hell.

THE TOOTH

Standing at the mouth of Orodruin, Frodo realizes he is ultimately incapable of destroying the Ring. Instead he puts it on his finger and disappears. The resolution is brought about by Gollum, who assaults the invisible Frodo, bites off his finger to get the Ring and then stumbles into the chasm. After the Ring has been destroyed, Frodo invites Sam to forgive Gollum, as the task could not have been accomplished without his treason:

> '[...] do you remember Gandalf's words: *Even Gollum may have something yet to do.* But for him, Sam, I could not have destroyed the Ring. The Quest would have been in vain, even at the bitter end. So let us forgive him!' (*LotR* 983)

Unlike the Ringwraiths and Shelob, which are manifestations of collective shadow, Gollum symbolizes Frodo's personal shadow. As Sam notices, "the two were in some way akin and not alien: they could reach one another's minds." Given his age, Gollum (originally called Sméagol) may also be seen as Frodo's distant ancestor. We are told he originates from a race which was akin to hobbits; the crucial difference being that, unlike the hobbits of Frodo's era who for the most part regard rivers, seas and other bodies of water with deep misgiving, Sméagol's people loved the river and excelled in fishing and swimming. Frodo is an orphan whose father drowned; whereas Tolkien reminds us time and again of the pleasure Gollum takes in diving in deep pools. In this context, water symbolizes the chthonic forces in Nature, with which Sméagol/Gollum is apparently more closely acquainted than Frodo. Although Frodo's people live in comfortable holes in the ground, suggesting they still have not completely disowned their link with the Mother, they have apparently become hostile towards her more dangerous, distrustful aspects. On the other hand, Gollum's affiliation with the daemonic half of the Goddess is stated quite explicitly: while he has never consented to serve Sauron, he willingly serves and worships the Terrible Mother Shelob.[6]

Sméagol's inclinations may also symbolize his fascination with introspection:

> He was interested in roots and beginnings; he dived into deep pools; he burrowed under trees and growing plants; he tunnelled into green mounds; and he ceased to look up at the hill-tops, or the leaves on trees, or the flowers opening in the air: his head and his eye were downward. (*LotR* 66)

Tolkien seems to suggest, however, that unless it is conducted with a noble purpose such as Frodo's and with wise counsel such as Gandalf's,

---

[6] At the same time, as mentioned above, it may be argued that Sam serves the Goddess in her benign aspect, represented by Galadriel. The theory would explain why both Sam and Gollum are indispensable to Frodo for the fulfilment of his task; their archetypal dimension also explains a good deal of the dynamics between Sam and Gollum, and especially the fact that they cannot stand each other.

introspection may turn out to be fruitless or even disastrous.[7] Indeed what Sméagol reveals and unleashes in the darkness are his most negative traits: his envy and possessiveness, which motivate him to commit murder in order to claim the Ring.[8] In order to justify his act, he convinces himself that the Ring has rightfully come to him as his birthday present. The lie hints at a deeper psychological truth, as Gollum/Sméagol's acquisition of the Ring actually marks the birth of his dark, shadowy self.

In Tolkien's ethical system, the person who wants to use the Ring may initially even be motivated by good intentions, but these are soon thwarted by the Ring itself, which ultimately appeals to and brings to the fore one's egotistic drive for power. The power with which the Ring endows its bearer is apparently shadow energy, inherent in the suppressed contents of the psyche, which the Ring seems to be able to reclaim. In other words, the Ring seems to act like an evil matchmaker, arranging a marriage between the ego and the shadow on the unwholesome ground of a power trip. Soon enough, in such an alliance, the ego finds itself under the sway of the power it wanted to wield. As Gandalf explains, the Ring is "so powerful that in the end it would utterly overcome anyone of the mortal race who possessed it. It would possess him" (*LotR* 60).

C. Zweig and S. Wolf (1997:49) ascribe great importance and centrality to this psychic complex, which they call the *power shadow*. In various ways, the shadow character uses power to serve the ego, pretending to be its friend, whereas actually it is an enemy, "a demon hun

---

[7] R. Bly (1988:64) makes a similar conclusion regarding Conrad's *Heart of Darkness*. Because Marlow has taken serious responsibility for running his ship and for the lives of the people on board, he is capable of communicating with his shadow in a non-destructive way; whereas Kurtz, whose commitment to "enlightening the savages" is just a form of self-deceit, looks into his soul and goes mad.

[8] The first thing Sméagol notices after the act of murder (and putting on the Ring) is that his family can no longer see him. Again, one cannot help but remember Conrad and the protagonist of *Lord Jim*, who also seems to become invisible to his pious, conservative family after he betrays their – and his – ideal of conduct.

gering for satisfaction." Echoing Gandalf, the authors remark: "Soon, we do not have power; it has us."

Unlike Gollum, Frodo really receives the Ring as a birthday present from Bilbo, in the year when he comes of age; the date is 22nd September, the beginning of autumn, also symbolizing ripeness. It is essential, however, that alongside with the Ring Bilbo also bequeaths to Frodo his wisdom, his notion of the existence of One Road, which leads towards the place "where many paths and errands meet", where one becomes aware of larger responsibilities and willingly embraces some transpersonal service.

Bilbo's idea about the Road may be construed in relation to the Jungian archetype of the Self. As C. Zweig and S. Wolf explain,

> [...] the term Self denotes the "God within", the transpersonal realm within the personal life. The Self contains the potential for the totality of personality, including the shadow. An experience of the Self brings purpose and meaning to life, a connection to something larger than the individual ego [...] When one can hear the voice of the Self and learn to obey it, one walks and talks with authenticity.
> (Zweig and Wolf 1997:16)

At the council in Rivendell, it is clearly the voice of the Self which urges Frodo to undertake the terrible journey:

> A great dread fell on him, as if he was awaiting the pronouncement of some doom that he had long foreseen and vainly hoped might after all never be spoken. An overwhelming longing to rest and remain at peace by Bilbo's side in Rivendell filled all his heart. At last with an effort he spoke, and wondered to hear his own words, as if some other will was using his small voice.

> 'I will take the Ring,' he said, 'though I do not know the way.' (*LotR* 288)

As Frodo gradually discovers "the way" in which his quest will be accomplished, it turns out that in the moments of greatest crisis help and guidance will come to him from his own treacherous shadow, Gollum. The idea that a treacherous figure may turn out to serve a good purpose in the general scheme of things is not novel in literature or myth. Goethe's Mephisto says about himself, "I am the power that wants to do evil, but always ends up, in spite of myself, doing good." Likewise, C. Zweig and S. Wolf (1997:307) remind us that Jesus could not have completed his destiny without the betrayal of Judas.

Frodo's recognition and acceptance of this dark partner, however, come only gradually. His initial reaction to the shadow is very much in line with Jung's observations. When Gandalf first tells him the story about Sméagol, he responds with repulsion and absolute refusal to recognize any kinship between the despicable features of the Other and his own:

> '[…]. How loathsome!'
> 'I think it's a sad story,' said the wizard, 'and it might have happened to others, even to some hobbits that I have known.'
> 'I can't believe that Gollum was connected with hobbits, however distantly,' said Frodo with some heat. 'What an abominable notion!' (*LotR* 67)

Frodo feels a passionate urge to deny any kinship with evil both at the *personal* and at the *tribal* level. In his study *The Seven Story Tower*, Curtiss Hoffman (1999:178) discusses a tendency well documented in numerous mythological contexts, to remove "the cause of a morally questionable event from the sphere of responsibility of [one's own] culture." He calls this construction *displacement* and finds it closely connected to the Jungian notion of Shadow projection. Having disowned the "morally questionable" traits and projected them upon another person or group, we consequently tend to react to them with self-righteous indignation or even with the desire to annihilate the Other. Gandalf points out to Frodo, however, that such a course of action is short-sighted and unwise:

> 'I am sorry,' said Frodo. 'But I am frightened; and I do not feel any pity for Gollum.'
> 'You have not seen him,' Gandalf broke in.
> 'No, and I don't want to,' said Frodo. 'I can't understand you. Do you mean to say that you, and the Elves, have let him live on after all those horrible deeds? Now at any rate he is as bad as an Orc, and just an enemy. He deserves death.'
> 'Deserves it! I daresay he does. Many that live deserve death. And some that die deserve life. Can you give it to them? Then do not be too eager to deal out death in judgment. For even the very wise cannot see all ends.' (*LotR* 73)

Having internalized Gandalf's wise advice, Frodo spares Gollum's life and befriends the repulsive creature by offering him sympathy and understanding. For this moral effort, he is richly rewarded. The authors of *Romancing the Shadow* maintain that, as a rule, a positive and a negative trait of one's character are exiled into the personal Shadow together. If we muster the moral courage to mine the former from the darkness, the latter emerges as well, presenting us with a surprising gift.[9] The authors call it "the gold in the dark side" (Zweig and Wolf 1997:13). The theory is applicable to Tolkien's character: Sméagol, with his marvelous physical agility, his skills in climbing and diving, his

---

[9] Tolkien's symbolism is quite consistent here: indeed when Frodo first catches a glimpse of Gollum he is *in a mine*, walking through the dwarves' delvings in Moria.

keen sense of touch and smell, his hunter's instincts and ability to find "safe paths in the dark", becomes Frodo's ally; Gollum, the embodiment of the power shadow, an envious, possessive murderer, remains his enemy. While Gollum hungers for the Ring, Sméagol is hungry only for the "juicy sweet" fish.[10]

Robert Bly (1988:29-38) recognizes five stages in the development of one's relationship with the shadow. In the first stage, we project the undesirable and shameful traits upon someone else, and deny any kinship with them. This corresponds to Frodo's refusal to accept that Gollum is a hobbit. In the second stage, the projections begin to 'rattle' and we notice some troublesome inconsistency in our perception of the person or group we have labelled as the Enemy. This would correspond to the moment when Frodo starts feeling pity for Gollum and acknowledges his positive qualities, while at the same time becoming aware of his own moral wavering about the Ring. In the third stage, we resort to 'moral intelligence' to repair the rattle, using some simplified philosophical or ideological construct to help us justify and persist in our continuous animosity towards the Other. Frodo does call Gollum "an enemy" and says he is "as bad as an orc" (*LotR* 73), but with the help of Gandalf, he apparently moves on from this stage fairly quickly. In the fourth stage, we recognize our own diminishment as a consequence of disowning some valuable portions of the self; in the fifth, we attempt to retrieve or, as Bly poetically puts it, to eat our shadow. At the physical plane, it looks as if Gollum has eaten Frodo's finger; at the inner plane, it is actually Frodo who has eaten his own shadow, so that its outer manifestation no longer needs to exist and therefore disappears in the chasm.

Bly also points out that melancholy and sorrow are always the

---

[10] Alternatively one might prefer to stick to Sam's terminology and call the two halves Slinker and Stinker.

marks of retrieved shadow. "[T]he person who has eaten his shadow spreads calmness, and shows more grief than anger." He/she also shows greater wisdom in coping with ethical issues (Bly 1988:42). The authors of *Romancing the Shadow* maintain that shadow-work eventually carries one beyond the naïve phase in which the world is viewed as "all-good", and beyond the cynical phase in which it is viewed as "all-bad", towards the third phase, characterized by "a more nuanced perception of reality and a capacity to tolerate paradox and ambiguity" (Zweig and Wolf 1997:18). At the end of the novel, Frodo displays all these qualities, acting as a "sadder and a wiser man" and treating mercifully the fallen wizard Saruman and his henchmen who have attempted to take over the Shire. At the same time, however, it seems that Frodo's deep insight into reality and the complexity of human nature have left him quite disinclined to continue to participate in the world of action. Upon their dealing with the bullies, Merry points out to him that he won't rescue the Shire just by being sad. Frodo's departure for a timeless realm across the sea marks the final divorce of *vita contemplativa* and *vita activa*; still, the book he leaves behind, like Tolkien's own narrative, should be viewed as attempts at preserving the link.

NATASA TUCEV (b. 1968) has been working as a teaching assistant for Anglo-American Literature at the Faculty of Philosophy, University of Nis, since 1995. In 1999 she obtained the Masters degree in Philology with her thesis *Views on Poetry in the Works of Seamus Heaney from 1965-1985*. Notable articles include "Alienated Lives: Having as a Dehumanizing Mode of Existence in Caryl Churchill's *Owners*", Facta Universitatis, 2/9, 2002. (http://ni.ac.yu/Facta) and "A Migrant Solitude: Poetry and Transcendence in Heaney's *Station Island*", Multimediaverlag Slobodan Valovic, Maintal, 2004 (http://www.buch-valovic.de.vu/). More important books of translations include the rhymed translation of Coleridge's *Rhyme of the Ancient Mariner* (Intelekta, Valjevo, 1994) and G. G. Byron's *Child Harold's Pilgrimage* (Zavod za izdavanje udzbenika, Beograd, 2004). She has published one novel, *Buskers*, (Knjizevna omladina Valjeva, Valjevo, 1996) and assorted short stories, including the prize-winning anti-war story "Hail Mary" (Radio B92, Beograd, 1993).

References

BLY, Robert, 1988, *A Little Book on the Human Shadow,* San Francisco: Harper.

GRAVES, Robert, 1961, *The White Goddess,* London: Faber & Faber.

HOFFMAN, Curtiss, 1999, *The Seven Story Tower,* Cambridge: Perseus.

HUGHES, Ted, 1993, *Shakespeare and the Goddess of Complete Being,* London: Faber & Faber.

TOLKIEN, J.R.R., 1995, *The Lord of the Rings,* (one volume edition; first published 1954-55), London: Harper Colins.

WALKER, Steven, 2002, *Jung and the Jungians on Myth,* New York: Routledge.

ZWEIG, Connie and Steve Wolf, 1997, *Romancing the Shadow,* New York: Ballantine Books.

Mythic Space in Tolkien's Work
(*The Lord of the Rings*, *The Hobbit* and *The Silmarillion*)

JEAN-CHRISTOPHE DUFAU

Abstract

The recent filming of *The Lord Of The Rings* enabled neophytes to realize that one of the most down-to-earth and simultaneously enchanting aspects of Tolkien's universe was Middle-earth, the imaginary world that he created with faultless coherence both from a geographical and a historical standpoint. Yet if such coherence only worked at these two rational levels, would both the film watcher and the novel reader have been so powerfully entranced? Presumably not, insofar as only imagination and its medium – myth – are likely to involve so wide an audience. Once this is understood, we may ask how far Tolkien's space is mythic, but we shouldn't bring our questioning only this far, for then, we will also have to determine how this mythic essence leads to enchantment by delineating the concept of original space.

I

Each truly inquisitive yearning, that is to say each instance of an urge for self-knowledge, begins with a long skyward stare. The Tree is a vital element for most of the characters in *The Lord of the Rings*. Sam is grieved when he realizes that the Party Tree has been felled down by the ruffians who devastated the Shire. Gondor is fated to wane while no new scion of the White Tree has been found. Nevertheless, the characters that are most intimately linked to their trees are not Hobbits or Men but Elves, and it is easy to understand why. The Lothlórien trees are out of the ordinary. The *mallorn*'s branches are never bare since the decaying leaves only fall once the new ones have begun to grow. This vegetal fantasy suggests that Tolkien's tree is the path to an ontology of free intuition that shakes off the yoke of scientific ratiocination. Our role is not to pose as agronomists and say: "This cannot be." The ontological target aimed at by the *mallorn* is imagination because its name comes from a doubly foreign language (Elvish, which does not exist) that points to another reality, and also because the tree in itself is the agent of cosmic fantasy. "The tree seems indeed to be the most appropriate medium of any cosmic dreaming; it is the path of a new awareness, that of the voice that gives life to the universe"[1] (Brosse 1993:33). This other plane of existence establishes a narrow kinship between the quest-borne being and the tree as main path to cosmic fusion. The speaking universe warrants the fulness of meaning. That the Galadhrim built their dwelling-places on their *mellyrn* is sufficient testimony of such a fact. They can be said to inhabit their trees as a soul does its body – intimately and powerfully. Frodo, pronounced an Elf-friend by the intuition of Goldberry who had just made his acquaintance, is going through a similar experience. He is about to follow Haldir up the great *mallorn* of Cerin Amroth from where he will be able to see Caras Galadhon where Celeborn and Galabriel dwell and at this moment, he has a physical insight of the vibration of undivided cosmic life:

> Haldir had gone on and was now climbing to the high flet. As Frodo prepared to follow him, he laid his hand upon the tree beside the ladder: never before had he been so suddenly and so keenly aware of the feel and texture of a tree's skin and the life within it. He felt a delight in wood and the touch of it, neither as forester

---

[1] "L'arbre semble en effet être le support le plus approprié de toute rêverie cosmique; il est la voie d'une prise de conscience, celle de la voix qui anime l'univers."

nor as carpenter; it was the delight of the living tree itself. (*LotR* 370)[2]

Frodo's sensation is deeply physical because it resorts to feeling, the sense that brings the body and the object into close contact. This intensity of sensation leads Frodo to a simple, intuitive apprehension of the tree ("the life within it") as opposed to the more scientific approach that the forester or the joiner would be likely to favour. It is with redoubled certainty that Frodo rejects the notion of the tree as material ("forester", "carpenter") to embrace the life in motion that is expressed by the aspectual value of incompletion ("liv*ing*") and to enjoy a self that exists for its own sake ("the living tree *itself*") beyond representation. Frodo has heard the cosmos speak to him: "thanks to its privileged medium – the tree – the world becomes spontaneously intelligible and within himself/herself, the meditating person retrieves the origins, the source of all life"[3] (Brosse 1993:34). On the same day, Frodo and his companions are to be the guests of the Lords of the Galadhrim, who live at the top of the tallest *mallorn* in Caras Galadhon. Frodo is staggered by the hugeness of the *mallorn*:

> Upon the south side of the lawn there stood the mightiest of all the trees; its great smooth bole gleamed like grey silk, and up it towered, until its first branches, far above, opened their huge limbs under shadowy clouds of leaves. (*LotR* 373)

The feeling of crushing hugeness ("the mightiest", "great", "huge") is doubled by an invitation to fly up ("stood", "towered", "far above", "clouds") that is superlative insofar as the top of the tree is hidden not

---

[2] All references to *The Lord of the Rings* (*LotR*) are to the text of the second edition (Tolkien 1983).

[3] "le monde, grâce à cet intermédiaire privilégié qu'est l'arbre, devient spontanément intelligible, le méditant retrouve en soi-même les origines, la genèse de toute vie"

by mere branches but by "its *first* branches." This leaves us astounded by the incredible tallness of this tree. The Fellowship climbs up this tree not only to visit Celeborn and Galadriel but also because "Foliage always is an invitation to taking off"[4] (Durand 1984:395). In the Fellowship only Legolas is used to that kind of ascension, so Haldir tells the other members that climbing to the top will not be an easy thing:

> It is a long climb for those that are not accustomed to
> such stairs, but you may rest upon the way.
> (*LotR* 373)

The idea of a long route on which one can rest recalls the journey motif. There is nothing surprising about this, for the climbing of this *mallorn*, and of any tree, is an ontology in itself.

> The tree links the earth to the sky and through this
> path the meditating person can, aware or unaware,
> go up and down, rise from the dark subterranean
> matter where he was once born to the pure lucent
> energy that gives him life and by which he is attracted.[5] (Brosse 1993:35)

Frodo is such a meditating person. As a hobbit, that is to say as the inhabitant of an underground hole named "Bag End" (which implies there is no way out apart from the way in), he really belongs to "the dark subterranean matter." As an Elf-friend, he is attracted by them and we should not forget that to Tolkien, Elves symbolized the lucent beauty of Good as well as the psychic energy that tends towards transcendence. Frodo can also take the same path the other way round, going down towards the tree's roots, that is to say towards the origins of the cosmos:

---

4 "Toute frondaison est invitation à l'envol"
5 "Par le canal que lui offre l'arbre unissant terre et ciel, conscient et inconscient, le méditant peut monter et descendre, passer de la matière obscure et souterraine, d'où il est un jour issu, à la pure énergie lumineuse qui l'anime et vers quoi il tend."

> he feels the first stages of a genesis take shape within him again, as if going back into the past had given him the power of beholding the world in the process of its own making, a world which only the presence of the tree enabled him to live in.[6] (Brosse 1993:35)

As he was standing at the foot of the *mallorn* in Cerin Amroth, Frodo had perceived the origins of the world. He had sensed time changing its direction and going back towards its origins as if meaning to have him see and hear places that had ceased to exist for aeons:

> Frodo stood still, hearing far off great seas upon beaches that had long ago been washed away, and seabirds crying whose race had perished from the earth. (*LotR* 370)

The Cerin Amroth *mallorn* is no exception. The tree figure often recurs in Tolkien's works. Thus, to quote just another example, the White Tree of Gondor also reaches back to the origins of the world insofar as it is a scion of Telperion in Valinor, the realm of the Gods of creation. In this case, white is the metaphor that points to the diaphaneity of time and the consequent cosmic attainability of origins. Of course, the tree being here a metaphoric agent, its referent does not have to be vegetal: it can also be textual. From texture (as Frodo feels it with his hand) to *textus*, from the irregular motifs at the surface of the tree's bark to the quasi-dendromorphic interlacement of narration, there is but one step. Tolkien tells us about the genesis of *The Lord of the Rings* by using a metaphor of the same kind. In the foreword he writes:

> As the story grew it put down roots (into the past) and threw out unexpected branches. (*LotR* 10)

---

[6] "il sent se retracer en lui l'esquisse d'une genèse, comme si, ayant remonté le cours du temps, il avait acquis le privilège de contempler le monde en formation, un monde que la seule présence de l'arbre a rendu pour lui habitable."

Similarly, Hobbits love family trees when they are very intricate:

> They drew long and elaborate family-trees with innumerable branches. (*LotR* 19)

It seems clear that both Tolkien's narrative tree and the Hobbits' family trees serve to point at the tangibility of origins, but the purpose of the tree motif is not limited to that aim only.

> The passage of time does not disseminate individuals as long as they keep in touch with origins. In a way, the family tree denies that time flows by, or rather it transforms its evanescent character, it crystallizes it into stability.[7] (Jourde 1991:44)

Nevertheless, time cannot be content with preservation: it also wants to be enriched and to such an end the lucent transcendence of the tree is no longer enough. It then becomes necessary to descend much lower than to root level, and the passage through the long and winding dark of the labyrinth cannot be avoided.

II

The labyrinth may seem to be an evident symbol for an ontological quest if one remembers that to enter the labyrinth one must know a password. One word is required and if one knows it, access is provided to the meaning of being. Therefore, the thing at stake here is a language of being: whoever knows its foundation (the first word) will be granted insight into the rest. Standing before the Gates of Moria, Gandalf has to face a new problem. The text of the riddle inscribed on the gates seems

---

[7] "Le passage du temps ne disperse pas les individus tant qu'ils gardent le contact avec l'origine. D'une certaine façon, l'arbre généalogique nie l'écoulement du temps, ou plutôt il en transforme le caractère volatil, il le cristallise en ordre fixe."

to be "Speak, friend, and enter." Gandalf believes he has to find a mysterious word and begins to rack his brains to extract the countless passwords that he has learnt in his long wanderings, but in vain: the door remains closed. The solution looks ridiculously simple when he finds it. He was supposed to translate the inscription as "Say 'Friend' and enter." This is no overly subtle linguistic point but a truly syntactic problem. It is likely that the Moria Dwarves never used quotation marks, or Gandalf would have managed to open the door straightaway. Entering a Tolkienian labyrinth therefore amounts to questioning language, which is but another proof that the aim of the labyrinthine quest is indeed accessing a language of being likely to unfold aspects of our selves that usually remain hidden. Those who cannot find the password are not ripe enough. Anger and violence but help redouble this immaturity. In *The Hobbit*, the dwarves try to force the secret door to Smaug's lair open with their pickaxes:

> They had brought picks and tools of many sorts from Lake-town, and at first they tried to use these. But when they struck the stone the handles splintered and jarred their hands cruelly, and the steel heads broke or bent like lead. (*Hobbit* 199-200)[8]

It is interesting to notice that the stone returns the very thing that the dwarves have to offer, namely raw violence. One might say that the dwarves' failure mirrors their method. No inner enlightenment can be obtained by stinting on questioning. In *The Lord of the Rings*, Gandalf is furious when he realizes that none of the passwords he knows opens the Gates of Moria, but he cleverly puts his fury to good use:

---

[8] All references to *The Hobbit* (*Hobbit*) are to the text of the third edition (Tolkien 1981).

> Again Gandalf approached the wall, and lifting up his arms he spoke in tones of command and rising wrath. *Edro, edro!* he cried, and struck the rock with his staff. [...] Then he threw his staff on the ground, and sat down in silence. (*LotR* 325)

Throwing his staff on the ground, the wizard rejects his urge to dominate through thoughtless violence. This attitude will enable him to resume his questioning once more and to eventually find the answer. But even once the door is open, the quest-bound wanderer's pains do not end. One enigma often hides another. The key to the mystery of being is not safely deposited on a shelf behind the newly opened door, or even beyond a maze of corridors. Inner space – inside the labyrinth as well as inside oneself – is not similar to the rational space one finds in the outside world. It is an instance of utter Beyondness. In the darkness of Smaug's lair, Bilbo loses his landmarks and asks:

> Which is East, South, North, or West? (*Hobbit* 225)

His reference to the four cardinal points is significant. He pines for the rational space of the surface, where landmarks that can be counted (there are four of them) provide stability by establishing the link between geographic space and inner space. The trust that the narrator of *The Hobbit* feels for these landmarks is textually obvious in his attribution of a capital initial to each of them. On the other hand, no geographic space can survive in a dark labyrinth, and this is most true in the Moria maze, where space is not content with being simply obscure like in Smaug's lair. In Moria, searching for personal space can only bring disappointment, for Moria shelters an anti-space that baffles all attempts at self-location:

> There were not only many roads to choose from, there were also in many places holes and pitfalls, and dark wells beside the path in which their passing feet

> echoed. There were fissures and chasms in the walls and floor, and every now and then a crack would open right before their feet. (*LotR* 329)

Dissemination ("many") opens on a space of collapse ("holes", "pitfalls") and of fissure ("fissures", "chasms", "crack") that engulfs both the horizontal and the vertical dimensions ("in the walls and floor"). Even the ground, which usually provides a feeling of stability, can give way in Moria. The traveller is bound to lose whatever bearings he used to have. How could he find a language of being in such a place since the concept of language refers to a *system* of signs? How could a *system* be found within Beyondness, which precisely stands for the rejection of all systems? The self cannot evolve in collapse and breaking: it dies in such places. The Huorn wood fills the Riders of Rohan who survived the Battle of the Hornburg with dismay. The day before, an empty plain stretched before their eyes and the next morning it is covered with trees! Inside the wood, time and space are no less whimsical:

> the sky was open above and full of golden light. But on either side the great aisles of the wood were already wrapped in dusk, stretching away into impenetrable shadows. (*LotR* 569)

Day and night are no longer separate and space is just impenetrable shadow – "utter Beyondness, Beyondness as presence"[9] (Jourde 1991:135). The Rohirrim follow a path precisely cut out for them because the Huorns are the friends of the enemies of the Orcs, who were lost in the "impenetrable shadows". No one ever returns from the utter Beyond:

---

9   "l'Ailleurs absolu, l'Ailleurs comme présence"

> Wailing they passed under the waiting shadow of the trees; and from that shadow none ever came again. (*LotR* 565)

Noisy multiplicity ("Wailing they") gives way to absence ("none", "ever [...] again"). We do not even know whether the Orcs are dead or prisoners, or how they died if die they did. No corpse is to be seen in the Huorn wood. No rational comfort will be granted to the reader:

> 'What has become of the miserable Orcs?' said Legolas.
> 'That, I think, no one will ever know,' said Gandalf. (*LotR* 569)

Not even Gandalf the wizard can *enunciate* the Beyond dramatized by the Huorn wood. From this Beyond, only "far cries, and a rumour of wordless voices" (*LotR* 569) come out. They are instances of a crude muddle of sounds ("voices") devoid of meaning, a language the characteristics of which are confusion ("rumour") and primitiveness ("wordless"). And yet, surprisingly enough, this approximatively spatio-temporal chaos leaves room for potential metamorphosis. Lost in the maze of the Goblin tunnels in the Misty Mountains, Bilbo makes an important discovery, and the way he makes this discovery is no less important:

> His head was swimming, and he was far from certain even of the direction they had been going in when he had his fall. He guessed as well as he could, and crawled along for a good way, till suddenly his hand met what felt like a tiny ring of cold metal lying on the floor of the tunnel. (*Hobbit* 74)

The ring found by Bilbo is the One Ring around which the fate of Middle-earth revolves. How did Bilbo achieve this feat, thanks to which he will become a 'burglar' in *The Hobbit* and give the Wise their one chance of overcoming Sauron in *The Lord of the Rings*? By chance! When reason cannot succeed (Bilbo has lost his bearings), intuition takes over ("guessed"). One thing is certain, though: if Bilbo had not got lost in this dark labyrinth, he would never have found the Ring, and till the end of his adventure he would have remained the "grocer" mentioned by Gloin at the beginning of the book. Similarly, Gandalf the Grey had to fall into the abyss and die in order to change into Gandalf the White. Thus, in Moria as in the Goblin tunnels, the passage through the labyrinth can only be effected by losing the reassurance of rationality and yielding to intuition. The language of being thus acquired is the irrational language of Beyondness. Both Bilbo the 'provincial' Hobbit and Gandalf the learned wizard can benefit from the new possibilities it brings to their inner growth.

III

Nevertheless, intuition is not the being's sole resource. The tree and the labyrinth motifs may both appeal to the intuitive side of being in order to enable its opening-up; the town motif, however, works differently. It uses the linguistic means of representation. Yet how far is the town in Tolkien's works a proper means of representation of being? In fact, it is perfectly equal to such a task because it is an act of representation in itself. "The town inscribes civilisation in landscape. It is the most definite landmark of civilisation: the town implies the mastery, the humanization of space"[10] (Jourde 1991:135). Legolas describes Meduseld, the capital of Rohan, as an act of inscription:

> 'I see a white stream that comes down from the snows,' he said. 'Where it issues from the shadow of the vale a green hill rises upon the east. A dike and mighty wall and thorny fence encircle it. Within

---

[10] "La ville inscrit la civilisation dans le paysage. Elle en est la marque la plus nette: la cité, c'est l'espace maîtrisé, humanisé."

there rise the roofs of houses; and in the midst, set upon a green terrace, there stands aloft a great hall of Men. [...].' (*LotR* 529)

The town of Meduseld can really be said to be inscribed in the landscape, since Legolas locates it by referring to a river that flows down from the snowy mountains. Then, it is an act of inscription insofar as it is separated from the landscape by the wall that surrounds it. What is written lies 'within'. Gilbert Durand viewed the house motif as "a microcosmic reduplication of the material body as well as of the mental body"[11] (Durand 1984:277). Thus, in Meduseld, inscription is embodied by the roofs of the houses, of the places inhabited by the Rohirrim, of the bodies that enclose their beings. At the centre of the centre lies Theoden's hall ("a great hall of Men"). Theoden is the king of the Rohirrim and this instance of embedding, viewed as a quest for interiority, is another proof that the inscription theme inherent in the town motif metaphorizes the representation of being. Nevertheless, in a war-ridden world, there is no way for being to develop independently of doing. The two go side by side when Legolas and Gimli take a critical look at the state of Minas Tirith from an architectural standpoint and they both imagine how they could improve the city's looks:

> 'There is some good stone-work here,' he said as he looked at the walls; 'but also some that is less good, and the streets could be better contrived. When Aragorn comes into his own, I shall offer him the service of stonewrights of the Mountain, and we will make this a town to be proud of.'
> 'They need more gardens,' said Legolas. 'The houses are dead, and there is too little here that grows and is glad. If Aragorn comes into his own, the people

---

[11] "un doublet microcosmique du corps matériel comme du corpus mental"

of the Wood shall bring him birds that sing and trees that do not die.' (*LotR* 529)

As a Dwarf, Gimli stresses the importance of doing ("stone-work", "contrived", "stonewrights", "make") while Legolas the Elf rather cares for being ("gardens", "grow", "glad", "sing") thanks to which death ("dead") can be superseded by life ("do not die"). Legolas links life to the joy of living when he says "that grows and is glad": in this context, "and" almost has a causal value, but Legolas does not disregard doing for all that. When he says "The houses are dead," he provides another proof of the symbolic equivalence between house and body: a house is inanimate and so cannot die, but metaphorically, a house regarded as the husk of the seed of being becomes as mortal as being itself and thus Legolas highlights the importance of doing by viewing it as a means of protecting being. We see that the two notions do not stand against, but rather interplay with each other. Therefore, our approach of the town in Tolkien's works shall be based on a dialectic of being and doing. We will try to avoid drawing too clear-cut a line between those two notions or forcing them into predefined categories. Our aim shall rather be to determine how far several modes of interaction between those two notions could be likely to open new vistas to the ever-evolving Tolkienian being.

IV

In the tormented world of Middle-earth, the town is always fortified and therefore has to face a major dilemma the ontological dimension of which outstrips its strategic basis: must one simply be (i.e. shun the world) or must one act (i.e. open up to influences)? Minas Tirith is a town where written accounts of past lore may be consulted though they are jealously kept under lock and key by Denethor the Steward whose life is only a withdrawal into what used to be:

> 'For to me what was is less dark than what is to come, and that is my care.' (*LotR* 269)

Nevertheless, Minas Tirith does not confine itself to such a withdrawal into the past. As a town, it is open to trade:

> There Anduin, going in a wide knee about the hills of Emyn Arnen in South Ithilien, bent sharply west, and the out-wall rose upon its very brink; and beneath it lay the quays and landings of the Harlond for craft that came upstream from the southern fiefs.
> (*LotR* 780)

As regards warfare and more precisely the War of the Ring, Minas Tirith attracts all the Free People like a magnet:

> And so the companies came and were hailed and cheered and passed through the Gate, men of the Outlands marching to defend the City of Gondor in a dark hour. (*LotR* 801)

The opening is here obvious in the greetings that the inhabitants of the City offer the newcomers. The term "Outlands", though, could not point out more clearly that the City is considered as being 'the interior' while its fiefs are meant to be 'the exterior'. Therefore, Minas Tirith is both withdrawn into itself and open to the outside world. The case of Gondolin in *The Silmarillion* could not be more different. Gondolin is shut to the outside world by the order of King Turgon who considers that secrecy is the only way of protecting it against Morgoth's henchmen, and even the solidarity against the Enemy in the name of which Minas Tirith warmly welcomes its allies goes unheeded by the lord of Gondolin who decides to bury his head in the sand regardless of what is going to happen:

> Shut behind their pathless and enchanted hills they suffered none to enter, though he fled from Morgoth hate-pursued; and tidings of the lands beyond came to them faint and far, and they heeded them little. (*Silmarillion* 290)[12]

King Turgon means to protect his subjects against Morgoth and it will be long before the inhabitants of Gondolin set out to make war on the Dark Lord. The goal of such a withdrawal is the preservation of an extraordinary mode of being, profoundly Elvish in nature since faithful to the Valinorean origins of the High Elves:

> Through many long years none passed inward thereafter, save Húrin and Huor only; and the host of Turgon came never forth again until the Year of Lamentation after three hundred and fifty years and more. But behind the circle of the mountains the people of Turgon grew and throve, and they put forth their skill in labour unceasing, so that Gondolin upon Amon Gwareth became fair indeed and fit to compare even with Elven Tirion beyond the sea.
> (*Silmarillion* 150)

Nevertheless, if being seems to come first in the City of Gondolin ("grew and throve"), doing is not absent for all that ("skill", "labour unceasing"). It is indeed a representation of existence that parallels Minas Tirith's in its quest for origins. Only the means vary: Lord Denethor looked for historical truth while Turgon's craftsmen resort to a more architectural approach. In both cases, past times are the inspiration: "what was" for Minas Tirith and "Tirion beyond the sea" for Gondolin. The element that makes the two cities irremediably different from each

---

[12] All quotations from *The Silmarillion* (*Silmarillion*) are taken from the English paperback edition (Tolkien 1979).

other is the relationship that each one keeps with its way of being or of acting. In Minas Tirith, being allows for trade and solidarity, that is to say for other people, whereas in Gondolin, being withdraws into itself and repels outsiders. *In Minas Tirith, being and doing stand side by side on one level; in Gondolin, doing is subjected to being.*

V

It is quite natural that being and doing lead to the notions of presence and absence. He who resorts to action instinctively searches for presence within absence. In this context, the distinction between being and doing looks obsolete. There is always action going on, even in Gondolin the place of withdrawal par excellence, and presence and absence are the elements that truly give birth to those twin behaviours and to the importance that is granted to either. Gondolin and Minas Tirith are the scenes of quests. Arrival in Gondolin is mysterious and initiatory:

> And at last by the power that Ulmo set upon them they came to the hidden door of Gondolin, and passing down the tunnel they reached the inner gate, and were taken by the guard as prisoners. Then they were led up the mighty ravine of Orfalch Echor, barred by seven gates, and brought before Ecthelion of the Fountain, the warden of the great gate at the end of the climbing road. (*Silmarillion* 288-89)

Before Ecthelion allows or does not allow entrance into Gondolin, the being must find the opening of the cave, then the inner door, then the seven gates. Sent by Ulmo the Vala, Tuor will pass all the tests. The accomplishment of his quest is the centre that Gondolin is the scene of:

> Then Tuor looked down upon the fair vale of Tumladen, set as a jewel amid the encircling hills; and he

> saw far off upon the rocky height of Amon Gwareth
> Gondolin the great. (*Silmarillion* 289)

The vale of Tumladen lies within the mountains, Amon Gwareth rises within the vale of Tumladen and Gondolin was built upon Amon Gwareth. This may be viewed as a dramatization of a quest for the interiority of being. Yet another proof is to be found in the additional level of embedding provided by the city itself:

> in the courts of Turgon stood images of the Trees of old, which Turgon himself wrought with elven-craft; and the Tree which he made of gold was named Glingal, and the tree whose flowers he made of silver was named Belthil. (*Silmarillion* 151)

Thus, the goal of the quest is not Gondolin in itself but the representations of the Valinorean origins that it contains. These two trees, sculptured by Turgon himself, are reproductions of Telperion and Laurelin, which Yavanna had grown in Valinor. The representation of being is at the heart of doing as it is considered by the Gondolindrim. The City was built on "the island-hill that stood there of hard smooth stone; for the vale had been a great lake in ancient days" (*Silmarillion* 149) and Tolkien's universe is so coherent in its least imaginative details that this topos echoes Almaren, the Valar's first Creation:

> And there upon the Isle of Almaren in the Great Lake
> was the first dwelling of the Valar when all things were
> young. (*Silmarillion* 40)

We find the same metaphor: an island on an original lake. In Gondolin, the lake has dried up, the waters of birth have withdrawn but the city was built in this place to keep the memory of origins alive. This presence is invoked by topographic signs (the valley, the hill, the many gates) and artistic signs (Turgon's two sculpted trees). The latter are linked to kingship so closely that when Tuor is allowed entry into Gondolin, the first thing he sees is Turgon's trees. This chronology in discovery has a symbolic significance:

> he was brought at last to the Tower of the King, and looked upon the images of the Trees of Valinor. Then Tuor stood before Turgon son of Fingolfin, High King of the Noldor. (*Silmarillion* 289)

The King and representation ("images") are closely linked. We understand that Turgon is the very embodiment of presence when just after saying that the two trees are in his tower the narrator of *The Silmarillion* describes King Turgon in all his pomp, with his complete ancestry and title. In Minas Tirith there has been no king for a long time; many years ago Eärnur, last king of Gondor, died without offspring and yet the same closed-in initiatory architecture prevails. Gandalf is allowed into Minas Tirith because he knows "the passwords of the Seven Gates" (*LotR* 803). Going through the Seven Gates is an initiatory since labyrinthic process:

> For the fashion of Minas Tirith was such that it was built on seven levels, each delved into the hill, and about each was set a wall, and in each wall was a gate. But the Gates were not set in a line: the Great Gate in the City wall was at the east point of the circuit, but the next faced half south, and the third half north, and so to and fro upwards; so that the paved way that climbed towards the Citadel turned first this way and then that across the face of the hill. And each time that it passed the line of the Great Gate it went through an arched tunnel, piercing a vast pier of rock whose huge out-thrust bulk divided in two all the circles of the City save the first. (*LotR* 781-82)

Action as it is conceived in Minas Tirith reads the town as inner space protected by seven walls. Going through is here a relevant initiatory theme ("went through", "piercing"). It enables Gandalf to ride from one part of the city to another, and the fact that these parts are named "levels" is meaningful: from the base of the city up to its summit, going through the gates leads from the districts of the simple inhabitants to the sacred enclosure where Lord Denethor dwells. The going-through dimension is also reinforced by the arabesque motif, for the initiatory road "turned first this way and then that." This architecturally marked road ("the paved way") is inscribed in the landscape, in the mountainside where the City is embedded ("built", "delved into"): therefore, it is a *writing* of the quest for being, a writing that it is our task to decipher. What is the goal of the quest theme in this city? How far is the sacred enclosure at the summit likely to have an ontological value? First of all, it is whole whereas the rest of the city ("all the circles of the City save the first") is divided in two by "a vast pier of rock": therefore, it may represent a desire to reach completeness of being. Then, this last level shelters the White Tree, the scion of Telperion in Valinor. It is not a sculpture but a real tree, a truly organic memory of Gondor's remotely Elven origins. The problem is that the White Tree is dead, has been dead for centuries while the King of Gondor, the cornerstone of the unity of the City and, metaphorically speaking, of the completeness of being, is no more. He has been replaced by Stewards who deal with current affairs, but are of no use to a being bent on a spiritual quest. In fact, during the War of the Ring, the real centre of Minas Tirith is neither the King, nor Denethor the Steward, nor the White Tree but the top of Denethor's tower, where the Steward has secured a secret chamber in which he keeps the Palantir. Thanks to this spheric magic stone, a steadfast mind can see what is remote and force the Palantir to show him not chance images but the very things he wants to see. Huge willpower, though, is needed to master these visions and Denethor cannot hope to compete successfully against Sauron for the control of the Palantir. It is true that the Palantir gives the viewer an intoxicating feeling of recovering origins since it enables him to see very far in space as well as in time, yet, it is no less true that such visions make the boundary between reality and representation much harder to distinguish. In Gondolin the link between King Turgon and origins is straightaway presented as being mimetic ("images", *Silmarillion* 241), whereas in Gondor the thing and its representation tend to merge into one another, allowing for deceit of the most subtle sort. Besides, Denethor spies upon a foe who possesses immense willpower and perfect knowledge of how a Palantir works – Sauron, master of illusion and treachery, not named the Dark Power in vain. The Dark Power is the stronger by far and however great Denethor's willpower may be, Sauron will delude him into seeing only the things that will lead him to wild despair:

> He was too great to be subdued to the will of the Dark
> Power, he saw nonetheless only those things which
> that Power permitted him to see. (*LotR* 890)

Thus Denethor will be the first to see a fleet of ships with black sails sail up the Anduin towards Minas Tirith but Sauron will not allow him to ascertain that though these ships belong to the Mordor-abiding pirates of Umbar, they have been taken over and are sailed by Aragorn, the Dunedain, Legolas and Gimli who are bringing Minas Tirith the very reinforcements thanks to which it will be able to crush its enemies. The contrast between Denethor's arrogant certainty of being master of a truth inaccessible to others and the dimension of the mistake of which he is the unaware but fully responsible victim is simply staggering. Thus, in Minas Tirith, the original sign is marred by the Steward's fetishism and the quest is lost in the meanderings of the Beyond's anti-space. The being thus obtained causes despair and suicide. In Gondolin, the quest led to withdrawal into oneself but it enabled the self to be preserved for want of anything better. The town as initiatory element in Tolkien's works brings little encouragement indeed: whether it causes withdrawal into oneself (Gondolin) or degeneracy (Minas Tirith), it barely allows one to hope for even a glimpse into completeness of self.

VI

Tree, labyrinth, town: Tolkien's space is mythic insofar as it dramatizes the quest for being. Errantry in Middle-earth may be vertical and upward (the tree), vertical but downward (the labyrinth) or horizontal (the town) but in every instance its value lies in its originative quality, thanks to which the traveller can build his/her own experience of existence and access the metamorphoses that are available within the context of his/her journey. A character-by-character analysis of the effects of such initiatory errantries would yield interesting results, for it would enable us to ground our approach on a less theoretical basis by working on the fundamental themes of hope, despair and reconstruction. Such themes were indeed dear to the faithful Christian that Tolkien was in spite of the sometimes stifling dogma of Roman Catholicism.

JEAN-CHRISTOPHE DUFAU holds a PhD in English literature and works in the Jehan Bodel secondary school in Arras (France). In 2002 his thesis was published at the Presses Universitaires Du Septentrion and in the same year he gave four lectures in Arras: 'The space of foundation in Tolkien's works', 'Middle-earth, the space of imagination', 'The double', and 'Rooting in the topos'.

References

BROSSE, Jacques, 1993, *Mythologie des Arbres*, Paris: Editions Payot & Rivages.

DURAND, Gilbert, 1984, *Les Structures Anthropologiques de l'Imaginaire*, Paris: Bordas.

JOURDE, Pierre, 1991, *Géographies Imaginaires*, Paris: José Corti.

TOLKIEN, J.R.R., 1979, *The Silmarillion*, (edited by Christopher Tolkien), London: Unwin Paperbacks.

TOLKIEN, J.R.R., 1981, *The Hobbit*, London: Unwin Paperbacks.

TOLKIEN, J.R.R., 1983, *The Lord Of The Rings*, London: Unwin Hyman Limited.

Language, Lore and Learning in *The Lord of the Rings*

DIRK VANDERBEKE

> A note of music is either right or wrong – *absolutely*!
> Not even Time can alter that: music is God's art.
> (Antonio Salieri in Peter Shaffer's *Amadeus*)

Abstract

Within the framework of fantasy literature, aspects of magic may take on the garb of science and serve as functional explanations of the principles and laws by which the world is governed. This raises the question of how knowledge about the world and its natural laws is acquired, used, transmitted or hidden. Knowledge, of course, is inevitably connected with language, and the basically creationist origin of Tolkien's world indicates the existence of a true language with a non-arbitrary form of signification, the knowledge of which equals the knowledge of the world and its underlying principles. The quest for true knowledge then turns into a kind of archaeological endeavour, piecing together the fragments of ancient language and lore, while the search for new knowledge is inevitably destructive and thus linked to evil. This presentation of knowledge unquestionably adds to the internal coherence of the texts, but undermines all claims that Tolkien's work might offer useful solutions to pressing modern problems, as the premises of his fictional world and ours are ultimately irreconcilable.

The relationship between magic, science and knowledge in general has for centuries been marked by the dichotomy of right vs. wrong, and even if recent science studies, in the wake of constructivist concepts, attempt to show that science's truth claims are ill-founded, this has hardly led to a revival of academic belief in pre-scientific modes of knowledge. In contrast to some attacks (and a few esoteric interpretations) Paul Feyerabend in his *Against Method* never demanded that "Equal weight [...] should be given to competing avenues of knowledge such as astrology, acupuncture and witchcraft" (Broad 1979:534),[1] but rather argued that reasonable and useful knowledge can exist on the basis of false premises and that some of that knowledge was unfortunately discarded with the advent of modern science (cf. Feyerabend 1993:78 fn). Over the last decades quite a few studies have explored the explanatory power and functionality of early modes of knowledge, e.g. Georgio de Santillana's and Hertha von Dechend's *Hamlet's Mill. An Essay Investigating the Origins of Human Knowledge and Its Transmission Through Myth.*[2] Moreover, it may be useful to bear in mind that the almost universal discredit of magic may be based on a distorted image of pre-scientific knowledge and on the unreserved acceptance of the present paradigms.[3] Keith Thomas has pointed out that:

---

[1] In this quote, the inclusion of acupuncture with astrology and witchcraft associates a serious, and by now widely accepted, medical treatment with the epitomes of superstition, a nice rhetorical trick which makes it just so much harder to fully contradict the statement.

[2] In his book on *Tolkien's World*, Randel Helms argues that "[w]e know, we modern rationalists, that myth contains no real 'knowledge' (at least as we now define the term), yet when we deflate and discard myth, we find gaping holes in our defences against the cold terrors of pain and death" (Helms 1974:57). This strict disregard for knowledge as transmitted by mythology may need to be revaluated while, of course, the claim that modern science was well capable of destroying earlier truth but failed to offer similar forms of consolation is almost a stock item in romantic critique of science. Santillana and von Dechend point out that "[t]he science of astrophysics reaches out on a grander and grander scale without losing its footing. Man as man cannot do this. In the depth of space he loses himself and all notions of his significance. He is unable to fit himself into the concepts of today's astrophysics short of schizophrenia. Modern man is facing the inconceivable. Archaic man, however, kept a firm grip on the conceivable by framing within his cosmos an order of time and eschatology that made sense to him and reserved a fate for his soul" (Santillana and von Dechend 1999:5-6). Peter Ackroyd has argued along similar lines in his novel *First Light* (1989).

[3] It may be necessary to stress here that this is not intended as an argument for scientific relativism. I merely want to point out that people of all times have been able to achieve useful knowledge within their respective world views, even if those world views were founded on erroneous premises. Thus any condescension towards previous modes of knowledge is ill-founded, in particular if one takes into account that at present the gap between those who are well informed about the most recent scientific paradigms and those who are not may well be wider than at earlier times.

> At all times most men accept their basic assumptions on the authority of others. New techniques and attitudes are always more readily diffused than their underlying scientific rationale. [...] Most of the millions of persons who today would laugh at the idea of magic or miracles would have difficulty in explaining why. They are victims of society's constant pressure towards intellectual conformity. (Thomas 1991:774)

The true/false-dichotomy informs the perspective of James George Frazer's *The Golden Bough*, unquestionably one of the most influential books on magic in the early 20th century and undoubtedly well-known by Tolkien. Frazer argues that magic is founded on the same basic presuppositions as science:

> [I]ts fundamental conception is identical with that of modern science; underlying the whole system is a faith, implicit but real and firm, in the order and uniformity of nature. The magician does not doubt that the same causes will always produce the same effects, that the performance of the proper ceremony, accompanied by the appropriate spell, will inevitably be attended by the desired result [...]. (Frazer 1996:56)

The problem, then, is not one of the premises but of their validity:

> The fatal flaw of magic lies not in its general assumption of a sequence of events determined by law, but in its total misconception of the nature of the particular laws which govern that sequence. (Frazer 1996:57)

Thus the difference is ultimately dependent on the outcome:

> It is therefore a truism, almost a tautology, to say that all magic is necessarily false and barren; for were it ever to become true and fruitful, it would no longer be magic but science. From the earliest times man has

> been engaged in a search for general rules whereby to turn the order of natural phenomena to his own advantage, and in the long search he has scraped together a great hoard of such maxims, some of them golden and some of them mere dross. The true or golden rules constitute the body of applied science which we call the arts; the false are magic. (ibid.)

In a more recent text we find a suitable abbreviation of Frazer's dictum: "Science is magic that *works*" (Vonnegut 1988:137, italics in the original). And indeed, if we look at the flights of fancy offered as possible achievements of magic there is little doubt that they have by now become part of our daily life – and in some suitably equipped modern housing the command "Let there be light" may well bring forth the desired result.[4]

In consequence, a literature depicting worlds in which magic actually works need not radically depart from our understanding of knowledge and how it is achieved and distributed. A replacement of the principles nowadays understood to be laws of nature by an alternative set of rules – e.g. the Law of Similarity and the Law of Contact and Contagion (cf. Frazer 1996:12-14) – might well yield a presentation of knowledge and research almost similar to our own experience. But in fantastic literature it hardly ever does, and additional aspects are usually interwoven with the depiction of fantastic worlds – including, of course, the world of *The Lord of the Rings*.

One of the questions that call for exploration when dealing with knowledge and magic in fantasy literature is the degree of difference from the laws underlying our universe and/or scientifically informed

---

[4] Actually, several of the perennial objectives of magic were also mentioned as programmatic goals of science in Bacon's *New Atlantis* or the list added to this text, e.g. flight, the prolongation of life, the curing of diseases counted incurable, the making of new species, the altering of features etc. (cf. Bacon 1986:245 and 249), they resurface in early science fiction and have, of course, since then been realized.

creations of possible futures. The existence of dragons, dwarves, trolls or orcs does not present a real problem, and similar beings regularly appear in the vast field of science fiction. Similarly, objects like the *palantíri*, the seven seeing stones, or Galadriel's mirror have a long pedigree in literature ever since Lucian described his voyage to the moon and the mirror of the Selenites:

> There is a large mirror suspended over a well of no great depth; any one going down the well can hear every word spoken on our Earth; and if he looks at the mirror, he sees every city and nation as plainly as though he were standing close above each.
> (Lucian, Book I)

By far not all accounts of such devices are strictly fantastic,[5] and by now there is, of course, no longer anything wonderful about "far seeing" devices. A rule of thumb concerning the principles governing a fantastic world might be, in how far they violate the most fundamental laws of everyday physics such as, for example, the Second Law of Thermodynamics.[6] Thus a fantasy story in which a castle is created from nothing by a jinn is different from one in which it is raised overnight by dwarves or fairies, a tale in which dead warriors arise differs from one in which dragon seeds grow into men, even if the function of the detail within the narrative is identical.[7]

---

[5] Edward William Lane describes a magical ceremony in the course of which a boy looks into the "ink mirror" and, to Lane's puzzlement, accurately describes various persons he had never seen, among them Lord Nelson as one-armed (cf. Lane 1890:251-252).

[6] Other fundamental laws like the speed of light as the maximum speed or the impossibility of action over distance are less relevant here, as, in contrast to science fiction with fantastic elements, the distances in question are too small to bring up the issue.

[7] This, of course, is only relevant in recent texts; the physics in question was of no concern to mythological times or the creators of the Arabian Nights, and thus all

From this perspective, there is little real magic in Middle-earth or, differently put, magic is divorced from the supernatural and has turned into an ambivalent term for a particular kind of knowledge that is available to some but not to others.

> 'Are these magic cloaks?' asked Pippin [...]
> 'I do not know what you mean by that', answered the leader of the Elves. 'They are fair garments, and the web is good, for it was made in this land. They are elvish robes certainly, if that is what you mean. [...]'
> (*LotR* 390)[8]

Similarly Galadriel rejects the hobbit's use of the word, in particular as it does not differentiate between the moral aspects of the practice or devices. She says about her 'mirror':

> [T]his is what your folk call magic, I believe; though I do not understand clearly what they mean; and they seem also to use the same word of the deceits of the Enemy. (*LotR* 381)

Magic thus appears to be in the eye of the beholder, i.e. it is the knowledge or craft that is unavailable or beyond the grasp of the respective speaker. Arthur C. Clarke formulated a similar idea in his famed Third Law: "Any sufficiently advanced technology is indistinguishable from magic" (quoted from Aldiss and Wingrove 1988:281). But neither 'magic' nor the knowledge or power of the wise, be they good or evil, can violate or change any of the rules of the world as laid down by Ilúvatar with the creation of the world. Moreover, in *The Lord of the Rings* as in the bulk of *The Silmarillion* the Godhead is absent and does not inter-

---

cases were equally miraculous, but for modern authors who resurrect those images the difference may well be significant.

[8] All quotations from *The Lord of the Rings* (*LotR*) are taken from the one-volume edition of 1978 (Tolkien 1978).

fere with the world. The situation is thus not unlike the one in England at the beginning of modern science, when the premises of religion and the belief in the first creation of the world by the supreme Godhead (as opposed to some medieval heretical concepts according to which the world was actually created by the devil) were still almost universally upheld, but Protestantism rejected the 'Catholic' idea of divine intervention by miracles or responses to prayers.[9]

In consequence, the powers of the wise are restricted in *The Lord of the Rings*. When the fellow travellers retreat from Caradhras and Legolas wishes that Gandalf would walk before them with a bright flame and melt a path in the snow, the 'magician' replies: "If Elves could fly over mountains, they might fetch the sun to save us. [...] But I must have something to work on. I cannot burn snow" (*LotR* 309). Similarly, even the mightiest force of evil, Melkor, second in power only to Ilúvatar himself, cannot truly create but only distort, and thus it is said about the coming of the orcs:

> The Shadow that bred them can only mock, it cannot make; not real things of its own. I don't think it gave life to the orcs, it only ruined them and twisted them; and if they are to live at all, they have to live like other living creatures. (*LotR* 948, cf. also *S* 58)

---

[9] In consequence, prayers for God's help and the deliverance from poverty, disease or other forms of plight were condemned by radical Puritans as a form of magic. "For those Protestants who believed that the age of Christian miracles was over, all supernatural effects sprang from either fraudulent illusion or the workings of the Devil" (Thomas 1991:304). The Calvinist doctrine of strict predetermination actually supported the belief in immutable natural laws, and thus "Protestant tendencies unwittingly helped to create an atmosphere favourable to science" (Hill 1997:25). Tolkien was, of course, a devout Catholic and saw *The Lord of the Rings* as a "fundamentally religious and Catholic work" (Letter to Robert Murray in 1953, quoted in Turner 2001:18), but as he left out "practically all references to anything like 'religion', to cults and practices, in the imaginary world" (ibid.), the link with Catholicism, in which practices like the sacraments are far more important than in Protestantism and the hope for divine intervention may well bring the desired result, is weakened.

Not only the laws of nature were laid down at the beginning of time, but, in analogy to Protestant and especially Calvinist doctrine, the world is also, at least to a major extent, predetermined. Future historical developments were already enacted and revealed when in the music of the Ainur the coming ages of Valar, Elves and Men and the threefold process from harmony to disharmony and strife that would later unfold were enfolded in the three great musical movements performed before the seat of Ilúvatar (cf. *S* 15-18).[10] The idea is to some extent akin to certain cabbalistic concepts, according to which the Torah as the history of the chosen people existed in a different form prior to the creation of the world (cf. Scholem 1973:90-105).[11] Then, again, the creation first by song and then in substance may bear some resemblance to the doctrine of the two books of God, the Bible and the material world. But in *The Lord of the Rings* the first language is non-verbal, ideal, and it belongs to the realm of the Godhead. Moreover, the knowledge about the future has not been fixed in scripture. In consequence, it is available only to those present at the first enactment, and since then it has trickled down from the Valar and Maiar to those who came later in world history. Within this world there are only remnants of this ideal first lan-

---

10 Paul H. Kocher (2000a) explored the problems of predetermination and free will in 'Cosmic Order'. But as this essay is taken from his book *Master of Middle-earth: The Fiction of J.R.R. Tolkien*, first published in 1972 and thus before the publication of *The Silmarillion*, he had to rely on the information given in *The Lord of the Rings* and the appendices alone. In consequence, Ilúvatar and the music of the Ainur are not mentioned and all conjectures about the One who designed the history of Middle-earth remain necessarily vague. In 'A Mythology for England', a passage from *A Reader's Guide to The Silmarillion*, reprinted in Bloom 2000, he only stresses that Tolkien "believed passionately in free will" (Kocher 2000b:105) but does not return to his earlier – very convincing – arguments about a world that nevertheless seems to be preordained.

11 The close link between the Torah and the world is also stressed in the *Babylonian Talmud* when Rabbi Ishmael tells Rabbi Judah, the scribe of the Torah: "My son, be careful, because thy work is the work of Heaven; if thou omittest a single letter or addest a single letter, thou dost as a consequence destroy the whole world" (*Babylonian Talmud*, 'Tractate Sotah', 2004:Folio 20a).

guage in which the knowledge has been revealed, and song appears as the equivalent of the occult language of magic, by which things can be done with words.

In particular, Tom Bombadil, the First, "older than the old" (*LotR* 282), seems to be in possession of that language, and his music gives him power over nature and protects him from the dangers within historical times. There have been discussions about his specific ontological status within the world of Middle-earth (is he a Vala, a Maia, a Nature Spirit, or some other supernatural being?), and no conclusive solution to the question seems to be possible (cf. Jensen 2004). Here I want to suggest that he is akin to an Adam without the fall: immortal, still living in a local Paradise and still in command of the divine and uncorrupted language that coincides with the essence of things. In the Bible, Adam is the one to give names to birds and beasts, "and whatever the man called every living creature, that was its name" (*Gen* 2.19). According to Walter Benjamin, Adam's act of naming indicates that the paradisical language of man must have been one of perfect knowledge (cf. Benjamin 1980:152), i.e. these names are not arbitrary significations but the 'true' ones which capture the essence of the named. A trace of this perfect act of naming can be detected in *The Lord of the Rings*, when Tom Bombadil gives names to the ponies of the hobbits: "Merry [...] had not given [the ponies] any such names, but they answered to the new names that Tom had given them for the rest of their lives" (*LotR* 159).

As in the Bible, the first language later differentiates into a variety of languages which poetically may strive to find the most appropriate names without ever achieving this ultimate objective. Thus the Noldor "were changeful in speech, for they had great love of words, and sought ever to find names more fit for all things that they knew or imagined" (*S* 69).[12] Finally, the multitude of languages in the Third Age resembles

---

12 All quotations from *The Silmarillion* (*S*) are from the 1978 edition (Tolkien 1978).

the arbitrary and interchangeable modes of signification after Babel – the 'ethnological' taxonomy of language is, of course, reminiscent of Nordic mythology and, in particular, of the 'Alvissmal' in the *Poetic Edda*. The ethnic roots of the languages may then express themselves in some onomatopoeic quality, and Legolas says about the language of the Rohirrim that "it is like to this land itself; rich and rolling in part, and else hard and stern as the mountains" (*LotR* 530).

The history of language thus resembles the three ages, and this development from the non-verbal language of Ilúvatar and the Valar to the poetic language of the elves and the pragmatic languages of humans, dwarves etc. may just possibly be akin to the three stages of language – the languages of gods, heroes and men – as described by Giambattista Vico in his *New Science*. According to Vico, "the language of the gods was almost entirely mute, only very slightly articulate; the language of the heroes, a mixture of articulate and mute [...]; the language of men, almost entirely articulate and only very slightly mute" (Vico 1984a:149). Moreover, the language of the heroes was emblematic and poetic,[13] and thus we find a development from the non-verbal to the poetic to the abstract quite similar to the one described by Tolkien.

This in itself may not seem too enlightening, but the approach to science and knowledge favoured by Vico also bears some analogy with the one depicted by Tolkien. Vico's text is to some extent an alternative to the new scientific methods in the aftermath of Bacon's programme[14] and their realisation by institutions like the Royal Society in England, which gave rise to the mechanistic world view and ultimately the Industrial Revolution, a fact that may be of considerable importance to the work of Tolkien. The possibility of conclusive research into the

---

[13] "[...] in the world's childhood men were by nature sublime poets" (Vico 1984a:71).

[14] In a paragraph of the second edition of the *New Science* that was left out of the third edition, Vico points out that his discovery is just the opposite of Bacon's (cf. Fisch's preface to Vico 1984a:xli).

true workings of nature is doubted by Vico with the argument that man can only understand what he has brought forth. As the material universe was created by God, its properties will in the final consequence always escape our attempts of theoretical understanding.[15] Vico's programme is thus chiefly concerned with all social aspects of human life, in particular with the origins of nations, their institutions and languages, as this is where their true nature can be discerned; the foremost 'faculties' of the new science are, in consequence, history and philology.

In Tolkien's world, 'good' knowledge is inevitably found in the past. It is covered by the term 'lore', and some aspects of the definition given by the *OED* are relevant here:

> 5. That which is learned; learning, scholarship, erudition. Now only *arch.* and *Sc.* (in the form *lair*, lear). Also, in recent use, applied [...] to the body of traditional facts, anecdotes, or beliefs relating to some particular subject; chiefly with attributive n., as *animal, bird, fairy, plant lore*. In the *Gentl. Mag.* for June, 1830, p. 503, a correspondent suggested that Eng. compounds of *lore* should be substituted for the names of sciences in *-ology*: e.g. *birdlore* for ornithology, *earthlore* for geology, *starlore* for astronomy, etc.

In Middle-earth, the unnamed correspondent's suggestion seems to have been taken up, and it is said of Radagast that he is "a worthy Wizard, a master of shapes and changes of hue; and he has much lore of herbs and beasts, and birds are especially his friends" (*LotR* 275). Moreover, 'lore'

---

[15] "[...] *geometrica demonstramus, quia facimus; si physica demonstrare possemus, faceremus. In uno enim Deo Opt. Max. sunt verae rerum formae, quibus earundem est comformata natura.*" (Vico 1984b:40, "We prove the geometrical because we bring it forth; if we were able to prove the physical we would bring it forth. For only in God the Almighty are the true forms of things that make up nature", my translation).

chiefly consists of traditional, i.e. old, facts and knowledge, and, in general, knowledge is found less in observation than in scriptures or legends of yore. Thus it is said of the hobbits:

> A love of learning (other than genealogical lore) was far from general among them, but there remained still a few of the older families who studied their own books, and even gathered reports of old times and distant lands from Elves, Dwarves, and Men. (*LotR* 15)

Similarly Celeborn advises the company that they should not "despise the lore that has come down from distant years; for oft it may chance that old wives keep in memory word of things that once were needful for the wise to know" (*LotR* 394). There may well be a residue of high truth in old wives' tales or "fables that Men have made as true knowledge fades (*LotR* 462-3). This fading of true knowledge is matched by a decline in the respect for knowledge among the men of Middle-earth for "in these days men are slow to believe that a captain can be wise and learned in the scrolls of lore and song [...] and yet a man of hardihood and swift judgment in the field" (*LotR* 797).

But an interest in old lore may not be sufficient, as at least some of the writings in the archives of the past have become almost incomprehensible, and Gandalf points out that in the archives of Minas Tirith there lie "many records that few now can read even of the lore-masters, for their scripts and tongues have become dark to men" (*LotR* 269).

Foucault's famed "archaeology of knowledge" gains a new meaning when research is concerned with the quest for and investigation into the oldest, most valid, but also least accessible information about the nature of things and the world in general. Not only do the wise in Tolkien's universe show an almost unrestricted bias for the Ancients over the Moderns, there has also been a continuous loss of knowledge over history. In consequence, the remnants of medicine that still exist in Gondor have been preserved from a greater earlier human knowledge about cures and healing, indicating that, as usual in Tolkien's book and fantasy literature, the sciences and skills of the past by far surpass those of later ages.

> For though all lore was in these latter days fallen from its fullness of old, the leechcraft of Gondor was still wise, and skilled in the healing of wound and hurt, and all such sickness as east of the sea mortal men were subject to. Save old age only. For that they had found no cure; and indeed the span of their lives had now waned to little more than that of other men, and those among them who passed the tale of five score years with vigour were grown few, save in some houses of purer blood. (*LotR* 894)

Similarly the craft as practised by the dwarves has at least to some extent dwindled. Glóin confesses that:

> [I]n metalwork we cannot rival our fathers, many of whose secrets are lost. We can make good armour and keen swords, but we cannot again make mail or blade to match those that were made before the dragon came. Only in mining and building have we surpassed the old days. (*LotR* 245-246)

The decline of knowledge and craft not only affects the mortals but also the major 'global players', who also seem to have lost access to the more glorious past.

> [The making of the *palantíri*] is beyond [Saruman's] art, and beyond Sauron's too. The *palantíri* came from beyond the Westernesse, from Eldamar. The Noldor made them. Fëanor himself, maybe, wrought them, in days so long ago that the time cannot be measured in years. But there is nothing that Sauron cannot turn to evil uses. […]

> Perilous to us are the devices of an art deeper than we possess ourselves. (*LotR* 621)

Moreover, science frequently takes up the garb of ethnology, as it is bound up with the history of the various peoples of Middle-earth.[16] Thus knowledge about mining and metallurgy is part of Dwarf-lore while botany belongs to Elven-lore. Even nature seems to obey the rule of ethnological association: When Frodo is wounded by the knife of the Nazgûl king, Aragorn first points out that "[f]ew now have the skill in healing to match such evil weapons" and then adds about the remedy that

> it is a healing plant that the Men of the West brought to Middle-earth. *Athelas* they named it, and it grows now sparsely and only near places where they dwelt or camped of old [...]. (*LotR* 214)

But Glóin's statement about the craft of the dwarves also points to another problem, i.e. knowledge is hardly ever freely distributed but usually carefully guarded and kept secret, adding to the loss of knowledge that is frequently bemoaned in the many jeremiads on the snows of yesteryear. Even useful or necessary information is withheld by those who are in the know, and Gandalf works on a strict "need-to-know" basis when dealing with the hobbits. Thus Pippin is unaware of the nature and dangers of the *palantíri* – Gandalf's condescending claim that knowledge "would not have lessened [his] desire, or made it easier to resist" (*LotR* 622) sounds weak in the face of the hobbits' dread of anything having to do with Sauron or Mordor. Knowledge is commonly passed, if it is passed at all, only to the initiated – e.g. from wizard to wizard – or to the next of kin, and thus it is lost with the death of a group of insiders, the decline

---

[16] In consequence, some of Gandalf's most relevant knowledge derives from his special field of interest, and he claims that "Among the Wise, I am the only one that goes in for hobbit-lore; an obscure branch of knowledge, but full of surprises" (*LotR* 62).

of an ethnic community, or the end of a family line.

On the other hand there is, of course, also new knowledge and 'research', however this is almost invariably linked to evil. From the very first attempt to introduce something new, original and individual into the world – when Melkor wove some of his own ideas into the music of the Ainur[17] – the new is almost coterminous with disruption, distortion and decline. In a world originally conceived as harmonious, any intrusion is a disturbance, a cause for imbalance, and thus by nature disharmonious.

In *LotR* it is chiefly Saruman who follows the path of innovation. However, it seems as if he were less interested in the production of new knowledge than in the exploitation of new technologies which invariably resemble the most evil aspects of industrialization. His achievements are chiefly in the creation of new machinery at the expense of nature[18] and in the organization of alienated work. In the words of Treebeard: "He has a mind of metal and wheels; and he does not care for growing things, except as far as they serve him for the moment" (*LotR* 494). In consequence, Isengard now resembles an industrial city in the 19th century:

> Once it had been green and filled with avenues, and groves of fruitful trees, watered by streams that flowed from the mountains to a lake. But no green thing grew there in the latter days of Saruman. The roads were paved with stone-flags, dark and hard. [...] The shafts ran down by many slopes and spiral stairs to caverns far under, there Saruman had treasures, store-houses, armouries, smithies, and great furnaces. Iron wheels revolved there endlessly, and hammers

---

[17] Melkor's original "desire of Light" (*S* 35) may well carry some notion of Lucifer, the bringer of light.

[18] The destruction of nature and its beauty is right from the beginning not only a side effect of evil machinations but their very objective, e.g. Melkor's slaying of the trees Telperion and Laurelin (cf. *S* 88-89).

thudded. At night plumes of vapour steamed from the vents, lit from beneath with red light, or blue, or venomous green. (*LotR* 578)[19]

Machinery here is almost synonymous with pollution. Moreover Saruman's work is chiefly concerned with tools for destruction and armoury.

> When Saruman was safe back in Orthanc, it was not long before he set some of his precious machinery to work. [...] Suddenly up came fires and foul fumes; the vents and shafts all over the plain began to spout and belch. Several of the Ents got scorched and blistered. (*LotR* 591)

The transformation wrought upon Isengard is later repeated in the Shire, and Sam gets a first glimpse of what is to come when he looks into Galadriel's mirror:

> Sam noticed that the Old Mill had vanished, and a large red-brick building was being put up where it had stood. Lots of folk were busily at work. There was a tall red chimney nearby. Black smoke seemed to cloud the surface of the mirror. (*LotR* 382)

After the hobbits return they have to face the reality of Sam's vision:

> Take Sandyman's mill now. Pimple knocked it down almost as soon as he came to Bag End. Then he brought in a lot o' dirty-looking Men to build a bigger one and fill it full o' wheels and outlandish contraptions. [...] They're always a-hammering and a-letting out a smoke and a stench, and there isn't no peace

---

[19] The shafts that run deep down to underground caverns with thudding machinery also recall the bleak vision of the world of the Morlocks in H.G. Wells's *The Time Machine*. At this point the dystopian science fiction and the romantic horror of technology coincide.

even at night in Hobbiton. And they pour out filth a purpose; they've fouled all the lower Water, and it's getting down into Brandywine. (*LotR* 1050-51)

These descriptions at first glance might be taken as no more than a severe critique of unrestricted industrialization and the terrifying living conditions of the working classes, and as a call for ecological considerations in the face of pollution. The new masters' hypocritical demands for "fair distribution" (*LotR* 1050) might then be read as an attack on socialist or communist governments, akin to the dystopian views presented in Orwell's *Animal Farm* or *1984*.

However, in the depiction of Saruman, there is more at stake than merely a vision of capitalist or socialist economies at their worst; hidden within the narration, modern science as such is challenged, and it may be useful to take a look at the passage in which Gandalf tells about his encounter with the master wizard when the latter finally revealed his true colours:

> 'I looked then and saw that his robes, which had seemed white, were not so, but were woven of all colours, and if he moved they shimmered and changed hue so that the eye was bewildered.
> "'I liked white better," I said.
> "'White!" he sneered. "It serves as a beginning. White cloth may be dyed. The white page can be overwritten, and the white light can be broken."
> "'In which case it is not longer white," said I. "And he that breaks a thing to find out what it is has left the path of wisdom." (*LotR* 276)

Gandalf's last line echoes Wordsworth's famous romantic critique of modern science from the poem 'The Tables Turned':

> Sweet is the lore which Nature brings;
> Our meddling intellect
> Mis-shapes the beauteous forms of things: –
> We murder to dissect.
> (Wordsworth 1994:481)

But more important is the example chosen by Tolkien, for the passage refers to one of Newton's major discoveries – white light can be split up into the rainbow colours – and thus it links Saruman's turn to evil to the beginning of modern science. Tolkien quite obviously shares not only William Blake's horror of the "dark Satanic mills" (Blake 1994:279; cf. also Helms 1974:74) but also his loathing for the whole scientific enterprise of which Newton had become the paradigmatic figurehead. In contrast to the laws of motion and the law of gravity, the splitting of light is not a particularly powerful tool in the course of mechanization and industrialization – moreover, the rainbow colours are usually regarded as rather pleasing and not as 'bewildering' to the eye. The selection of this example thus stresses the critique of all artificial intervention into nature, and while the beauty of the natural rainbow may well be celebrated, the research into optics disrupts and breaks the pre-existing harmony of pure white light.

But then, of course, to 'break' light is a metaphor, if by now a dead one, and in taking it as literal and transferring it to things in general, Gandalf moves on to criticise a reductionist science in favour of a holistic approach. The assumption that we cannot understand things by analyzing their parts indicates that the whole is more than the sum of its parts, a concept frequently employed not only by recent research into emergent systems, but also in all fields of esoteric knowledge. Saruman, on the other hand, stresses that the world as it is serves only as a starting point, and thus his work intends to alter nature as we know it. In the world of Tolkien, this is necessarily fallacious, for true knowledge is concerned with the 'whole', while the striving for new knowledge is invariably accompanied by the destruction of the perfect balance within this 'whole'.

Within a mythological world, created by a supreme Godhead and organized according to some original perfect harmony, the recovery of this perfect past, of the Golden Age that has always been lost in myth, may well be the ultimate objective of any hero's quest. A similar idea can be found once more in the cabbala, i.e. in the concepts of *zimzum* and *tikkun*, according to which it is the perennial task for every human being to work towards the healing of the primordial split that originally took place within the Godhead itself and then was repeated in the breaking of the vessels, in the severance of light and darkness, land and sea, man and woman, and, finally, tree and fruit (cf. Scholem 1973:148-157). In such a world it is possible that a complete body of useful knowledge existed, but was lost, and that the archaeology of knowledge may then lead to a recovery of lore that is superior to any attempt at new research and analysis. However, once this longing for a glorious past is transferred from myth to the problems of our world, the nostalgic approach to knowledge and the unreserved bias for the Ancients over the Moderns turns from a romantic vision to a reactionary and a-historical fantasy.

The introduction of pressing modern problems into the imaginary world of Middle-earth indicates that Tolkien like so many authors enriched his fantastic creation with social and political criticism; and it has frequently been argued that "the action transpiring in [Tolkien's] world have symbolic relevance to some of the profoundest issues of our age" (Helms 1974:58) or that "our response to Tolkien's myth is an honest guide to our own – and society's – reality" (Evans 1972:202).[20]

---

[20] Rose A. Zimbardo adds a turn of the screw and endorses Tolkien's loathing of science and the project of enlightenment in general, arguing that "a vision of cosmic harmony – the great *discordia concors* – [...] was celebrated in English literature until the mid-seventeenth century, when men – even poets, who should have known better – discarded that image [...] and, in the spirit of Saruman, set up their own rea-

In contrast, Jenny Turner points out that Tolkien's work fails to capture any reality outside its own fixed limits.

> The lore is self-referential, centripetal, an occult system. As astrology is to physics or conspiracy theory to history, so Middle-earth is to literature and learning. It's a closed space, finite and self-supporting, fixated on its own nostalgia, quietly running down. (Turner 2001:24)

Undoubtedly, Tolkien fulfilled one of the main requirements that every author of fantasy literature faces: "his creation must seem consistent within itself, following observable laws and demanding, through its own proof, that we believe in it" (Evans 1972:27). But while the presentation of knowledge and its sources unquestionably adds to the internal coherence of the imaginary world, it also effectively cuts off this world from the one we live in. The solutions to the problems evoked in the text work only if the premises are also valid, i.e. that the past is inherently better than the present and that in that past a full body of knowledge existed of which new approaches and new modes of knowledge and learning are only distortions and perversions. The fact that hope in Tolkien's world is based on the rejection of new ideas and of a scientific approach in general distinctly lessens its power to offer the reader more than an escapist vision[21] or a jeremiad for the legends, lore and learning of old.

---

son as their god and launched us into the dark ages from which we are still struggling to emerge" (Zimbardo 2000:133). In consequence, she fully embraces not only Tolkien's nostalgia for a pre-enlightenment era but also his imagery when she turns from criticism to sermon and preaches that: "We are each of us 'Ring-bearers', for the smallest but most important of the 'rings' that the great Lord of Rings holds is each creature's idea of self" (Zimbardo 2000:136).

[21] This is not merely the repetition of a critique frequently – and often erroneously – levelled at fantastic literature. Tolkien seems to have regarded an imaginary escape from the modern age as something inherently worthwhile (cf. Helms 1974:16-17).

DIRK VANDERBEKE studied German and English Literature at the University of Frankfurt/Main, from where he also received his doctorate degree in English Literature in 1994. His doctoral thesis, *Worüber man nicht sprechen kann* (*Whereof One Cannot Speak*), deals with aspects of the unrepresentable in philosophy, science and literature. His habilitation study, *Theoretische Welten und literarische Transformationen* (*Theoretical Worlds and Literary Transformations*) examines the recent debate about 'science and literature' and science's role(s) in contemporary literature. In addition, he has published on topics as diverse as Joyce, science fiction, self-similarity, and vampires. Recently he has co-edited an annotated edition of the German translation of James Joyce's *Ulysses*, published in celebration of the Bloomsday centenary. Dirk Vanderbeke has taught at the University of Wisconsin – Milwaukee, the University of Frankfurt/Main, Widener University in Chester, PA, and at the University of Greifswald.

References

ALDISS, Brian and David Wingrove, 1988, *Trillion Year Spree. The History of Science Fiction* (first edition 1986), London et al.: Paladin.

BABYLONIAN TALMUD, 8/11/2004, 'Tractate Sotah', Folio 20a, translated under the editorship of Rabbi Dr. I. Epstein, http://www.come-and-hear.com/sotah/sotah_20.html.

BACON, Francis, 1986, *The Advancement of Learning and New Atlantis* [1605/1627], ed. Arthur Johnston, Oxford: Clarendon.

BENJAMIN, Walter, 1980, 'Über Sprache überhaupt und über die Sprache des Menschen' (first published 1916), *Gesammelte Schriften* II.1, Frankfurt: Suhrkamp, pp. 140-157.

BLAKE, William, 1994, 'Selections from Milton' (engraved 1804-1809), in *The Works of William Blake*, Ware, Hertfordshire: Wordsworth Editions, pp. 279-290.

BROAD, William J., 1979, 'Paul Feyerabend, Science and the Anarchist', *Science* 206, 11/2/1979, pp. 534-537.

EVANS, Robley, 1972, *Writers For the Seventies: J.R.R. Tolkien*, New York: Thomas Y. Crowell.

FEYERABEND, Paul, 1993, *Against Method* (rev. 3rd edition, first edition 1975), London und New York: Verso.

FRAZER, James George, 1996, *The Golden Bough*, abridged edition (first published 1922), New York: Touchstone.

HELMS, Randel, 1974, *Tolkien's World*, Boston: Houghton Mifflin.

HILL, Christopher, 1997, *Intellectual Origins of the English Revolution Revisited*, Oxford: Clarendon.

JENSEN, Steuard, 8/11/2004, 'What is Tom Bombadil', http://tolkien.slimy.com/essays/Bombadil.html.

KOCHER, Paul H., 2000a, 'Cosmic Order' (from *Master of Middle-earth, The Fiction of J.R.R. Tolkien*, 1972), in Harold Bloom (ed.), *J.R.R. Tolkien: Modern Critical Views*, Philadelphia: Chelsea House, pp. 11-25.

KOCHER, Paul H., 2000b, 'A Mythology for England' (from *A Reader's Guide to The Silmarillion*, 1980), in Harold Bloom (ed.), *J.R.R. Tolkien: Modern Critical Views*, Philadelphia: Chelsea House, pp. 103-111.

LANE, Edward William, 1890, *An Account of the Manners and Customs of the Modern Egyptians* (reprinted from the 3rd edition 1842), London et al.: Ward, Lock and Co.

LUCIAN, 8/11/2004, *The True History* (2nd century A.D.) (*Verea historiae*, translated by H. W. Fowler and F. G. Fowler), http://oddlots.digitalspace.net/guests/lucian_true_history.html.

SANTILLANA, Giorgio de, and Hertha von Dechend, 1999, *Hamlet's Mill. An Essay Investigating the Origins of Human Knowledge and Its Transmission Through Myth* (first published 1969), Boston: Nonpareil.

SCHOLEM, Gerschom, 1973, *Die Kabbala und ihre Symbolik* (first published 1960), Frankfurt: Suhrkamp.

THOMAS, Keith, 1991, *Religion and the Decline of Magic* (first published 1971), London: Penguin.

TOLKIEN, John Ronald Reuel, 1978, *The Lord of the Rings* (first published 1954-1955), London: Unwin (quoted as *LotR*).

TOLKIEN, John Ronald Reuel, 1979, *The Silmarillion* (first published 1977), London: Unwin (quoted as *S*).

TURNER, Jenny, 2001, 'Reasons for Liking Tolkien', *The London Review of Books*, 11/15/2001, pp. 15-24.

VICO, Giambattista, 1984a, *The New Science of Giambattista Vico* (*Scienza nuova*, 3rd edition 1744, translated by Thomas Goddard Bergin and Max Harold Fisch), Ithaca and London: Cornell University Press.

VICO, Giambattista, 1984b *De nostri temporis studiorum ratione* (first published 1708), Darmstadt: Wissenschaftliche Buchgesellschaft.

VONNEGUT, Kurt, 1988, *Cat's Cradle* (first published 1963), Harmondsworth: Penguin.

WORDSWORTH, William, 1994, *The Works of William Wordsworth*. Ware, Hertfordshire: Wordsworth Editions.

ZIMBARDO, Rose A., 2000, 'The Medieval-Renaissance Vision of *The Lord of the Rings*', in Harold Bloom (ed.), *The Lord of the Rings: Modern Critical Interpretations*, Philadelphia: Chelsea House, pp. 133-139.

The Lord of the Rings in the Wake of the Great War: War, Poetry, Modernism, and Ironic Myth

MARTIN SIMONSON

Abstract

This paper takes a look at the influence of World War I on the literary imagination in general, and on Tolkien's creations in particular. The aim is to take a closer look at an aspect of *The Lord of the Rings* which has not been much studied: its relationship to what Northrop Frye calls "ironic myth". For this purpose, Tolkien's best known work will be compared with some of the poetry written by poets who took part in the First World War, and with three well known writers of 'high modernism'.

It is surprising how little critical work has been devoted to analysing Tolkien's literary production in its historical context, given its vast implications.[1] In this paper I will stress the importance of World War I and its effects on the literary imagination in general, and on Tolkien's creations in particular. By comparing his work with the general tendencies of the so called war poets – Wilfred Owen, Edward Thomas, Siegfried Sassoon and Robert Graves among others – on the one hand, and of three of the most renowned writers of "high modernism" – Ezra Pound, T.S. Eliot and James Joyce – on the other, I hope to shed some light on

---

[1] Apart from Shippey's (2003) tentative approach to the literature of Tolkien in the context of modernism, Rosebury (2003) includes a chapter on the same subject in his *Tolkien: a Cultural Phenomenon*, while Garth (2003) deals more specifically with the effects of the First World War on Tolkien's imagination and literary production. However, none of these writers touch very deeply, if at all, on Frye's theory of modes as a means of connecting the work of Tolkien with some of the major impulses present in high literary modernism.

an aspect of *The Lord of the Rings* which has seldom been delved into very deeply: its relationship to what Northrop Frye calls "ironic myth".

The starting point of this paper will be the views of two critics on the literary production during and after the First World War, Paul Fussell (1975) and Modris Eksteins (1990). The former dedicates the main body of his study, *The Great War and Modern Memory*, mostly to the effects of life in the trenches on the production of the so-called "war-poets". Fussell argues that war-time behaviour associated to natural events, such as stand-to at sunrise and sunset, or a contemplation of the sky from the "grave" – perspective of the trenches, was frequently used as motifs by the poets in a conscious attempt to find some sort of traditional meaning in the war which would help them making sense of it. Furthermore, the idea of the enemy as a constant presence, a threatening element ready to attack at any moment, would, in Fussell's view, condition a strongly dichotomized world view reflected in what he calls the "versus habit". The simplifying oppositions good/bad, day/night, friend/adversary, etc., found in much of the WWI poetry, would be a consequence of this. Fussell also considers other effects of the war, such as nostalgia for the Edwardian age as a result of the soldiers conceiving time in terms of "before" and "after" the war.

In addition, the inability to communicate the terrible and bewildering experiences in the trenches would lead to an extensive use of the pastoral, as an antithesis of the infernal sceneries, supported in turn by a strong English tradition in pastoral poetry. Given the extensive reading and literary learning of most soldier poets, they would be relying on the literary canon in order to establish an intelligible ground for their poetry, by way of ironic allusion. In this context, the literary quest romance, notably the versions of it presented in the Victorian pseudo-medieval romances of William Morris – Fussell (1975:135) mentions *The Well at the World's End* as one of the most frequent sources of imagery for the soldiers – and in Bunyan's Christian allegory *The Pilgrim's Pro-*

gress, were particularly appealing. Likewise, military secrets, rumours and the general apocalyptic atmosphere in the trenches gave rise to a whole series of legends and superstitions that flourished during the war.

In general terms, the break with the "innocent" past and the following experience in the trenches is, according to Fussell (1975:82), accompanied by "the passage of modern writing from one mode to another" (in terms of Northrop Frye's well-known theory of modes), given that the writings of the war-poets describe a sense of transition, pointing both backward, towards the low mimetic mode, and forward, towards the ironic mode's return to myth.

Modris Eksteins, while writing largely on the same matter, provides us with a different focus in the more recent *Rites of Spring: the Great War and the Birth of Modern Age,* in which he discusses the influence of the war on the modernist movement. He acknowledges a general British pull towards the preservation of the social values of the Edwardian age – respectability, civility, dignity, controlled progress, etc. – as opposed to the German drift towards a questioning of the 19th century values and an urge to build a new civilization from the ashes of the previous one. The disillusion among the fighting men during the war would, in Eksteins' view, lead to a break with the past and to a new conception of the soldier, representing a creative force in the process of destruction and renewal. Eksteins (1990:214) argues that

> the horror had [...] little interpretative potential except in very personal terms, [and that the] signs and sounds of war are connected with an art in which the rules of composition were abandoned and provocation became the goal.

Quite in contrast with Fussell, Eksteins claims that an abandonment of conventional forms was seen as the most adequate aesthetic response to the experience. Another effect of the war, according to Eksteins

(1990:214), is that language as such lost its social meaning and became a more personal vehicle for the poets, and that irony was adopted as the natural mode for poetic expression.

Considering the writings of Pound, Eliot and Joyce in the light of these thoughts on the literary outcome of the Great War, we are presented with two distinctively different aesthetic responses to the conflict; one represented by those who fought in it, and another by those who witnessed it from the home front. While the tendency towards the use of irony and myth is shared by both "currents", it is commonly acknowledged that the so called "high modernism", to which Pound, Eliot and Joyce belong, is anti-historicist, that it rejects sequential time and absolute polarities, that it is elitist and exhibits a sense of cultural despair. Furthermore, moral relativism is a prominent feature, as is the attention to the cultural consequences of a technological society and the fascination with chaos and irrationalism – characteristics which have led some historians and literary critics to claim that the intellectual mood it created helped setting the scene for the rise of fascism in the decades following the war.[2] It was extremely technical – I would say almost *clinical* – in its use of language and emphasis on the precise word; it strove at creating self-referential narrative universes, and usually exhibited a vast literary erudition which was exploited partly in order to give coherence to the works by using the so called "mythological method".[3]

Broadly speaking, the mentioned authors looked upon history as being simultaneous with the present, and considered their times a transition – perhaps a perpetual transition.[4] Nevertheless, or perhaps just be-

---

[2] Cantor (1988).

[3] M. Bradbury and J. Macfarlane (1976) and N.F. Cantor (1988) offer two good introductory studies on Modernist literature and Modernism as a cultural response to the conditions of the 20th century.

[4] See Kermode (1968) on the literary effects of contemplating time as a perpetual transition.

cause of this, at this stage in history modern man grows very conscious of the cultural heritage of the past. Modernist writers tried to make sense of the present by incorporating a good deal of the literary canon into their respective works, juxtaposing the allusions and imitations with examples from modern life to create an ironic effect, using a kind of bricolage technique that fitted well their perception of modernity as a fragmented and heterogeneous state of affairs.

Frye (1971:62), in speaking of the narrative mode of ironic myth, mentions that cyclical theories of history helped rationalize the idea of the return to myth, alluding to Yeats and Joyce, among others. As we have mentioned before, the consciousness of being immersed in an age of transition was widespread among the modernists. The resulting mode, ironic myth, would seem to imply an encyclopaedic effort towards the incorporation of the total literary heritage of the past, ironically contrasted with the present. Myth as such, however, was often applied merely as a means of scaffolding, to provide a structure that would keep the apparently chaotic mixture of images together.

Joyce, in *Ulysses*, invented the method by using Homer's *Odyssey* as a constant reference in terms of structure, episodes, places and characters, as a means of compensating for the weakening of narrative structure and unity. As Gross (1974:9) says, Joyce pays great attention to words and to the power of language, illustrating just to what extent the world we live in is a linguistic product, and trying to "stress the need to get rid of the enslaving structures that language imposes on us." As a result, the reader is overwhelmed by references to all kinds of literary traditions. There is also a tendency in Joyce to use his own previous writings as significant references, having, among others, the protagonist of 'A Portrait of the Artist as a Young Man', Stephen Dedalus, reappear in Dublin after his flight to Paris, and this implies that we need to be familiar with the previous work in order to grasp the full meaning of the new.

Pound's approach to narrative tradition is largely the same: the whole canon should be seen as a simultaneous order, which new works of art may modify as they are incorporated. One of Pound's aims was to display the interrelations between the great works of art, judging them from a simultaneous standpoint. According to Witemeyer (1981:10-11), Pound's theory of the "Luminous Detail" stated that some details can reveal a whole epoch, and he tried in his poetry to disclose these instances of revelation and put them in relation to each other largely by the use of allusion (to provide ironic contrasts), imitation (to write in the "spirit" of some author) – and by using persons from history and literature as spokesmen. Inspired by Joyce's "mythological method", the structure of the *Cantos* is likewise based on Homer's *Odyssey*. The technique of self-referentiality is in Pound extended to the idea that every single part of his writings should be seen in relation to the whole body of his work, critique and poetry alike.

T.S. Eliot shared the idea of the simultaneous order with Pound, and it is perhaps in his poetry where literary reference is most conspicuous; "a literature of literature" as Aiken calls it (Cox and Hinchcliffe 1968:94). His symbols are drawn from myth, legend, literature and history, and once again used to provide ironic contrast. Brooks claims, however, that the surface parallelisms that in Eliot make ironical contrasts are matched by the surface contrasts that make parallelisms, and that the combination gives the effect of "chaotic experience ordered into a new whole" (Cox and Hinchcliffe 1968:157). This dichotomy is a tool that Eliot uses to renew and vitalize old symbols turned to clichés and thus emptied of meaning by excessive familiarity.

The main arguments against the effectivity of these works are based on their elitist character. Some parts of *Ulysses* only make sense if one is familiar with the corresponding autobiographical event, and the reader is often perplexed by the complexities, the seemingly irreconcilable contradictions and the sometimes arbitrary use of symbols. In the case of Pound, the reader must necessarily be aware of the poet's opinion of the sources referred to – and share them – for the "Luminous Detail" to work. As for Eliot, we need to be equally familiar with a large corpus of texts, references, languages and their implications in order for the poems to make sense, a task certainly not made easier by the abstract presentations. In response to these complexities, Craig claims that the limited public response to *The Waste Land* is an indication that it is not the representative work of the present age (Cox and Hinchcliffe 1968:212). The same could be said of *The Cantos* and *Ulysses*, works that likewise depend heavily on scholastic institutions for their reading.

If the criterion of public response is the one feature that determines a literary work's representability of an epoch, then J.R.R. Tolkien's *The Lord of the Rings* would qualify as one of the most representative.[5] But it might qualify as such on other grounds, too. Considering Tolkien's work in the context of the Great War will enhance our understanding of its contemporary character. Having served as a soldier at the front, Tolkien was exposed to largely the same conditions as the war poets, which, among other things, is reflected in his treatment of "the enemy"; certain sceneries, such as the Dead Marshes and the wasteland beyond; the pastoral, clearly English conception of the Shire, set in an Edwardian kind of rural bliss; the use of the quest motif and inspiration from the narrative dynamics of Victorian pseudo-medieval romances; the structure of the work showing a movement from idyllic rural life towards technological destruction and a subsequent urge to renew the lost idyll; the use of mythical elements and a general, elegiac mood, etc.

One example that shows well the change in mentality that occurs in times of transition is the poetry of the hobbits, which illuminates the

---

[5] One of Shippey's (2003) arguments for proclaiming J.R.R. Tolkien "the author of the century" is his enduring popularity.

shift from innocence to fear and frustration. In this sense, it is similar to the change in Georgian poetry, a poetic movement sharing certain affinities with the romantic strain of the previous century, which began taking shape in the years before the Great War. I will try to show this with two examples. The first is a poem by Rupert Brooke, representative of the kind of carefree, jocose and even trivial attitude towards life, which we nowadays tend to associate with the Edwardian times. It is called *The Little Dog's Day*, and it deals with the adventures of a dog that makes a pact with the gods Odin and Thor, saying that the dog may do whatever it pleases during one day, as long as it agrees to die at the end of the day. Said and done, the dog provokes a terrible brawl, upsetting the whole village:

> He took sinewy lumps from the shins of old frumps
> And mangled the errand-boys – when he could get 'em
> He shammed furious rabies, and bit all the babies,
> And followed the cats up the tree, and then ate 'em![6]

Finally, the day ends and the dog dies, and that is the end of the poem too, which may be defined as a rather hilarious composition with a rural theme, expressed in a simple, quotidian and jovial language, which creates a folk-tale kind of atmosphere with a direct and unpolished humour, based on burlesque scenes and situations.

We find something quite close to this in Bilbo's song *The Merry Old Inn*, that Frodo sings at The Prancing Pony. *The Merry Old Inn* is about a rural inn that, one night, is visited by the Man in the Moon, who wants to try the famous local beer. At the inn there is a cat that plays the violin, a dog that makes jokes and a cow that dances. The Man in the Moon takes a slug of the beer and falls asleep under the table, thus

---

[6] Driver (1996:30).

endangering the arrival of the new day. The animals, inspired by the innkeeper, try to wake him up:

> Now quicker the fiddle went deedle dum-diddle;
>   the dog began to roar
> The cow and the horses stood on their heads;
> The guests all bounded from their beds
>   and danced upon the floor.
>
> With a ping and a pong the fiddle-strings broke!
>   the cow jumped over the Moon,
> And the little dog laughed to see such fun,
> And the Saturday dish went off at a run
>   with the silver Sunday spoon.[7]

The song ends with the Man in the Moon and his moon-cart back in the sky where they belong and the Sun coming up.

The burlesque situation, the jocose tone, the popular language, the exclamations and the use of natural cycles as a temporal framework make the similarities with Brooke's poem obvious. It is also significant that both poems were composed before the start of the conflict – the Great War and the War of the Ring – that changed these worlds, when it still made sense to write such poetry. The narrator of *The Lord of the Rings* even states, as an introduction to the song, that "Only a few words of it are now, as a rule, remembered" (Tolkien 1993:174).

The contrast with the poem *Roads* by Edward Thomas, another poet writing about matters of the English countryside who also participated – and died – in the Great War, is notable. This poem is marked by a pastoral and elegiac tone and it ponders the places to which roads may lead

---

[7] Tolkien (1993:176).

us, and their permanence beyond the brief scope of time that man spends on Earth:

> Roads go on
> While we forget, and are
> Forgotten like a star
> That shoots and is gone
>
> The next turn may reveal
> Heaven: upon the crest
> The close pine clump, at rest
> And black, may Hell conceal
>
> Often footsore, never
> Yet of the road I weary
> Though long and steep and dreary
> As it winds on forever

The poet then compares the roads of different mythologies, contrasting them with the present ones, which lead to France and the war:

> Now all roads lead to France
> And heavy is the tread
> Of the living; but the dead
> Returning lightly dance;
>
> Whatever the road bring
> To me or take from me
> They keep me company
> With their pattering.[8]

Thomas suggests that it is inevitable to follow roads, that time forces us to move on whether we like it or not, and that there is a kind of consolation in their durability, a transcendence beyond death which may ease

---

[8] Driver (1996:48-49).

the pain of the situation brought upon us by a particular historical moment.

The ambiguity of this poem, written after the beginning of the war, brings about an elegiac tone, which takes it far from the attitude expressed in poems such as *The Little Dog's Day*. In this, and in many other aspects, it recalls *The Road Goes Ever On*, another song that Frodo sings as the hobbits approach the borders of the Shire.

> The Road goes ever on and on
>   Down from the door where it began,
> Now far ahead the Road has gone,
>   And I must follow, if I can,
> Pursuing it with weary feet
>   Until it joins some larger way
> Where many paths and errands meet.
>   And whither then? I cannot say.[9]

Just like Thomas's poem, the song shows a very different attitude compared with the jolliness of Frodo's inn-song, or the bathing song that the hobbits sing at Crickhollow. This song also features a melancholy, almost elegiac tone: the hobbits will have to follow the road, leading them where it may. Frodo, who at that moment thinks he will be travelling east alone, suspects that he will leave his beloved Shire never to come back, and that the world, from this moment and on, will never be the same again. This is also what happens. Frodo does come back, but he is not the same as he used to be. The world has changed, and he has changed with it. Having been intimately associated with the Ring, and the Third Age, which ends with it, he disappears little by little from the narrative when his mission is accomplished.

---

[9] Tolkien (1993:86-87).

Frodo as a character reflects in a sense the disillusionment among many people after the Great War, an attitude which questions a basic cornerstone of spiritual welfare: is this world worth fighting for? Frodo seems to be affected by the same kind of transitory spirit, already before he knows that he will be going West with the elves.

However, we should bear in mind that Tolkien was not aiming at writing an allegory on the 20th century, but rather at constructing a tale with many layers of significance, providing it with a broad scope of applicability. He was, of course, conscious of the transitory spirit of the period, and of the cultural despair following in the wake of the Great War. With the modernists he shared a concern for the precise, accurate word and a profound respect for the creative power of language;[10] he exhibited a complex, though always coherent treatment of narrative chronology,[11] and created a vast body of self-referential literature. As in the cases of Pound and Joyce, his main work refers to other writings of his own, notably *The Hobbit* and *The Silmarillion*, for an enrichment of the narrative, though it never *depends* on them for understanding and cohesion. But the most striking feature of the *Lord of the Rings* is its new approach to the mode of ironic myth and the literary encyclopaedia that comes with some of it.

Traversi (1976:14) states that T.S. Eliot had to face a very difficult poetical task, because he needed to invent his own symbolical structures,

> rather as though Milton had needed to invent the story of the Fall before writing Paradise Lost or Dante to work out the details of his cosmic scheme before writing his poem.

---

[10] E. Segura (2004:33-34) explains in a simple and concise manner Tolkien's method of showing how a particular language defines the society speaking it.

[11] For one of the best explorations of Tolkien's narrative treatment of time and its relationship to modern philosophical and artistic views, see V. Flieger (1997).

This is, in fact, exactly what Tolkien does, but on a vastly more elaborate level compared with Eliot's poetry. His other works, such as *The Silmarillion* and *The Hobbit*, are referred to in the text, but not in the same way as in the modernist works we have looked at. *The Lord of the Rings* does not *depend* on a previous knowledge of certain sources for comprehension and coherence (though it is true that this knowledge *enriches* the narrative). When in *The Waste Land* or *Ulysses* we come across a quotation, the poet may or may not declare where it comes from, but in any case, the reader needs to be familiar with the work, the artist or the character referred to if the allusion is to be invested with any meaning. In *The Lord of the Rings*, the treatment is different. The references to previous traditions are in most cases integrated in a harmonious and natural way. The allusions to the literature or to historical events of Middle-earth are revealed to us through songs, poems or tales, well contextualized, and contribute to the coherence and depth of the world. This stands in contrast to the modernists' shaping of a world-vision with emphasis on fragmentation, absurdity and chaos by means of ironic juxtapositions. An example of how Tolkien integrates traditions in his narrative is when Sam, after hearing Aragorn mention the name Gil-galad in relation to Weathertop, the place that they are approaching, recites part of a song about this historical-mythological character. Aragorn then explains that it was not Bilbo who wrote the song, as Sam thinks, but that it is a part of the lay called *The Fall of Gil-galad*, composed in an ancient tongue. (Only a few pages later, Aragorn also sings the tale of Tinúviel, and when he has finished he gives a full account of the story's context).

This contextualization of references and allusions is, together with the absence of intentional irony, a fundamental feature of Tolkien's work that makes it very different from the creations of writers and poets such as Joyce and Eliot. It is a consequence of the voluntary invention of a secondary world, of which no reader can have previous notions.

The encyclopaedic strain in the literature belonging to the mode of ironic myth is as evident in *The Lord of the Rings* as it is in the modernists' work, and here too, we find a "return" to mythical structures and themes. As for the irony, Tolkien, in linking his work to modernity and its problems through the story's *applicability* – which I believe is achieved to a great extent thanks to the intertraditional dialogue present in the narrative – ensures effects that are similar to the ironic juxtapositions of the images of Eliot, Pound and Joyce, with the important difference that the irony is not intended, nor an internal part of the narrative, but *external* to it. References to our own world are not explicit, and we perceive the possible irony (an interpretation which in any case depends on the reader, not on the author's conscious attempt at conveying ironic contrasts) only when comparing Middle-earth with our own world and its present conditions. In this sense, in Tolkien's work we may also speak of contrasts that really are parallelisms, and parallelisms that become contrasts.

It seems clear that we should be able to consider *The Lord of the Rings* in the light of Frye's mode of ironic myth, given the similarities of technical procedures, themes and structures, among other things, with other works belonging to this mode. However, apart from the lack of intended irony, there are several other important differences. I consider that the most interesting of these differences is the natural ease with which Tolkien reflects the interaction between the different narrative traditions of Northern Europe. Apart from the smooth approach to this interaction, in *The Lord of the Rings* the different narrative traditions explore and question each other as they are merged, in a totally different way compared to the works of Joyce, Eliot and Pound.

In Middle-earth, as in the poetry of Pound and Eliot, our Western narrative traditions are presented as a simultaneous phenomenon.

Shippey (2003:249-250) claims that in *The Lord of the Rings*, Northrop Frye's five modes – myth, romance, high mimetic, low mimetic and irony – cohabit in the shape of different characters: Gandalf, Bombadil and Sauron belong to the mythic mode, Aragorn, Legolas and Gimli to romance, Boromir and Éomer to the high mimetic, most hobbits to the low mimetic and Sam and Gollum to the ironic. In creating a fantastic, self-referential setting, and using the story of *The Lord of the Rings* to portray it, Tolkien invented a literary chronotope capable of hosting the whole range of literary tradition, from myth through the epic, romance, the realist novel and on to the ironic, in which the different traditions are able to meet and influence each other in a new and revolutionary way compared with the modernist approach. The traditions simply become more flexible within the framework of Middle-earth and *The Lord of the Rings*. The characters, as they are affected by this inter-traditional dialogue, assimilate features of different traditions, which makes it impossible for us to consider them as belonging only to this or that narrative tradition.

Gandalf does assume a mythic stature at the bridge of Khazad-dûm, for instance, but he has been irritable throughout the episode of Moria due to more novelesque reasons: he has not been able to smoke as much as he would have liked to. Aragorn corresponds to a typical pattern of romance when he returns from exile, conquers the throne and makes the kingdom fertile again, but in Edoras he acts like a northern epic hero straight out of *Beowulf*, and at Bree, his figure is closer to the role of the helper-guide of Victorian imperial adventure novels. Boromir, it is true, receives a death similar to that of Roland at Amon Hen, but ever since Rivendell he has been presented as a warrior tormented by a very novelesque inner conflict. As for Frodo, he is the principal narrator of the story, and he is also the character who, during the course of the narration, assimilates most features of the different narrative traditions that interact in Middle-earth. As such, he emerges as the hero who carries the weight of narrative tradition, and from this point of view, the ring becomes a symbol of a cycle of Western literary tradition, which is coming to an end. The ring is destroyed, the Third Age concludes, a new epoch begins. Frodo's testimony of the events that illustrate the cycle's final stage – ironic myth – acquires characteristics of the whole body of narrative traditions, aiming back to myth by using the very feat of Frodo, and Aragorn's subsequent fertilization of the Kingdom of Gondor, as its central themes. Significantly, as the cycle is completed and the story ends, Frodo leaves Middle-earth, never to come back.

Creating a secondary world in which the different traditions are given space to interact with natural ease, Tolkien constructs a powerful alternative to high modernism in portraying the recapitulation of previous tradition implied by writing in the mode of ironic myth. He did not accept the aesthetics of modernism, nor the modern conditions of life, and put the fantastic world as such in contrast to the modern world without explicit references to modern life. Recreating instead of quoting, paraphrasing or imitating, and making use of creative allusion instead of ironical contrast, the references become much more accessible to the reader, the interaction between modes is made smoother, and the simple objects whose brilliance has been made dull by familiarity (which can be compared with Eliot's attempt at reinvigorating old symbols) are seen in a new light.

In this sense, *The Lord of the Rings* is a manifesto of a radical revision of the modernists' approach to ironic myth. As it happened, it turned out to be a highly popular one. This may or may not have to do with the ease with which the narrative traditions of the past interact in this work, but it is a fact that they do maintain a constant dialogue throughout the narration. The dynamics of this dialogue should be well worth a closer study, especially if we bear in mind that the modernist approach yielded a very limited popular response in comparison.

MARTIN SIMONSON took his degree in English Philology at the University of the Basque Country in Vitoria, Spain. He has recently finished his PhD dissertation at the same university, focusing his investigations on the narrative dynamics of *The Lord of the Rings*, especially on the way in which J.R.R. Tolkien constructs a narrative framework capable of hosting a great amount of different narrative traditions while at the same time performing a highly suggestive exploration of the limits of this 'intertraditional' dialogue.

References

AIKEN, C. 'An Anatomy of Melancholy', in Cox and Hinchcliffe (1968:91-99).

BRADBURY, M. and J. MACFARLANE (eds.), 1976. *Modernism*, (first edition), Harmondsworth: Penguin.

BROOKS, C., 'The Waste Land: critique of the myth', in Cox and Hinchcliffe (1968:128-161).

CANTOR, N.F., 1988, *20th Century Culture: Modernism to Deconstruction*, (first edition), New York: Peter Lang.

COX, E. and A.P. HINCHCLIFFE (eds.), 1968, *T.S Eliot: The Waste Land*, (first edition), London: Macmillan.

CRAIG, D. 'The Defeatism of The Waste Land', in Cox and Hinchcliffe (1968:200-215).

DRIVER, P. (ed.), 1996, *Early Twentieth Century Poetry*, (second edition, first edition 1995), London: Penguin Books.

EKSTEINS, M., 1990, *Rites of Spring: The Great War and the Birth of the Modern Age*, (first edition), New York: Anchor Books.

FLIEGER, V., 1997, *A Question of Time: J.R.R. Tolkien's Road to Faërie*, (first edition) Kent, Ohio: The Kent State University Press.

FRYE, N., 1971, *Anatomy of Criticism: Four Essays*, (first edition in paperback, first edition 1957), Princeton, New Jersey: Princeton University Press.

FUSSELL, P., 1975, *The Great War and Modern Memory*, (first edition), London: Oxford University Press.

GARTH, J., 2003, *Tolkien and the Great War: The Threshold of Middle-earth*, (first edition), New York: Houghton Mifflin.

GROSS, J., 1974, *Joyce*. (Translated from English by Marcelo Covián. Original title: *Joyce*, 1970), Barcelona: Ediciones Grijalbo.

KERMODE, F., 1968, *The Sense of an Ending: Studies in the Theory of Fiction*, (second edition, first edition 1967), New York: Oxford University Press.

ROSEBURY, B., 2003, *Tolkien: A Cultural Phenomenon*, (second, revised and enlarged edition, first edition 1992), Houndmills: Palgrave.

SEGURA, E., 2004, *El Viaje del Anillo*. Barcelona: Minotauro.

SHIPPEY, T., 2003, *J.R.R Tolkien: Autor del Siglo*, (translated from English by Estela Gutiérrez. Original title: *J.R.R. Tolkien: Author of the Century*, 2000), Barcelona: Minotauro.

TOLKIEN, J.R.R., 1993, *The Lord of the Rings*, (first published 1954-55; second edition 1966), London: HarperCollins.

TRAVERSI, D., 1976, *T.S. Eliot: the longer poems*, (first edition), London: The Bodley Head.

WITEMEYER, H., 1981, *The Poetry of Ezra Pound: Forms and Renewal 1908 –1920*, (first edition), Berkeley and Los Angeles, California: University of California Press.

'A Man, lean, dark, tall':
Aragorn Seen Through Different Media

CONNIE VEUGEN

Abstract

The release of the Peter Jackson film trilogy has renewed interest in both the original *Lord of the Rings* by Tolkien and in old and new adaptations of the book. Because of the film the character of Aragorn has, at least for the present-day film-going audience, become a prominent figure in Tolkien's *Lord of the Rings*. In this article I will illustrate how Aragorn is portrayed in the original work and how his character is shown in other versions across several media. As every medium has its own narrative techniques and technical limitations, I will use theories by Wendy Doniger and Northrop Frye to establish the fundamental elements of Aragorn's character. These will then be used to examine how well every adaptation has succeeded in portraying the essence of the character.

INTRODUCTION

Tolkien's *Lord of the Rings* trilogy[1] has long been considered impossible to adapt to other media. Tolkien himself found the work "unsuitable for dramatic or semi-dramatic representation" (*Letters* 255), and although Terrence Tiller, who adapted the books for the BBC Third Programme[2] corresponded with him, Tolkien did not enjoy this first dramatization

---

[1] I will abbreviate the full title to *LOTR*. I quote from the three volume 1974 paperback edition published by Allen and Unwin. The book titles will be abbreviated to *FR* (*Fellowship of the Ring*), *TT* (*Two Towers*) and *RK* (*Return of the King*). To distinguish between the main tale and the appendices I will refer to the appendices with the letter *A*. I will refer to the 2000 edition of Humprey Carpenters *The Letters of J.R.R. Tolkien* as *Letters*.

[2] This was the only adaptation made during Tolkien's lifetime. It was broadcasted in 1955 and 1956.

(*Letters* 228). This, however, has not deterred others from making their own version, using such diverse media as animated and live action film, a radio play and several computer games.[3] One of the most recent adaptations is Peter Jackson's 2000-2003 series of films which both spurred new interest in Tolkien's original work and which led to their own adaptations in the form of, amongst others, board games, trading card games, war games and computer games. As Jackson's adaptation is especially action oriented, the character of Aragorn has become one of the main protagonists even besting Gandalf.[4] In this article, I will compare the character of Aragorn as he is depicted in some of these adaptations. I will use Ralph Bakshi's 1978 animated film version, Brian Sibley and Michael Bakewell's 1981 radio play, Peter Jackson's 2000-2003 live action film trilogy and, finally, the official FELLOWSHIP OF THE RING[5] game produced by Vivendi. For brevity's sake I will limit the main comparison to the first encounter with Aragorn at the inn of the Prancing Pony in Bree. Before I do so, I will first introduce Aragorn as he is shown by Tolkien.

TOLKIEN'S ARAGORN

One inconvenience with the character of Aragorn is that Tolkien presents him both in the book and in the appendices, as he writes himself: "[T]he highest love-story, that of Aragorn an Arwen Elrond's daughter

---

[3] The earliest official computer game is a text adventure entitled LORD OF THE RINGS released in 1981 for the TRS-80 Model I home computer.

[4] Although it is a very crude method, a simple word count of the original texts shows that Frodo's name is mentioned most frequently with 1855 entries, followed by Sam with 1230 entries and Gandalf with 1076 entries. Even when adding the names Aragorn (707) and Strider (226), he only totals to 933.

[5] Both the whole work as well as the individual parts of the trilogy are often called the same in different media. To distinguish between them, I shall use *italics* for Tolkien's original, <u>*underlined italics*</u> for the radio play, SMALL CAPS for the film versions and *ITALIC SMALL CAPS* for the computer games.

is only alluded to as a known thing" (*Letters* 161). Even though he regarded it "the most important of the Appendices [and] part of the essential story" (*Letters* 237), he put it outside the book:

> Because it could not be worked into the main narrative without destroying its structure: which is planned to be 'hobbito-centric', that is, primarily a study of the ennoblement (or sanctification) of the humble. (*Letters* 237)

So, to fully understand Aragorn's motives, it is necessary to include the appendices and I will do so. I will use the Ring as reference for a short sketch of Aragorn's past since the finding of the One Ring not only triggers the Ring quest but also Aragorn's personal quest: his foretold role as heir of Elendil and Isildur and as future king of Gondor and Arnor, which in itself is closely tied in with the story of Aragorn and Arwen.

At the end of the Second Age, during the *Last Alliance* in the year SA 3441, Sauron is overthrown. His power departs when Isildur cuts the Ring from his hand:

> 'I [Elrond] beheld the last combat on the slopes of Orodruin, where Gil-galad died, and Elendil fell, and Narsil broke beneath him; but Sauron himself was overthrown, and Isildur cut the Ring from his hand with the hilt-shard of his father's sword, and took it for his own.' (*FR* 234)

By claiming the Ring,[6] Isildur turns it into an heirloom of the North Kingdom,[7] not knowing that it will cause his death:

---

[6] 'This I will have as weregild for my father and brother' (*FR* 234).
[7] 'The Great Ring shall go now to be an heirloom of the North Kingdom' (*FR* 242).

> 'But the Ring was lost. It fell into the Great River, Anduin, and vanished. For Isildur was marching north along the east banks of the River, and near the Gladden Fields he was waylaid by the Orcs of the Mountains, and almost all his folk were slain. He leaped into the waters, but the Ring slipped from his finger as he swam, and then the Orcs saw him and killed him with arrows.' (*FR* 58)

Eventually Isildur's inheritance Arnor, the kingdom of the North, "is broken up in princedoms and finally vanishes" (*Letters* 157). Isildur's line survives but they become "a hidden wandering Folk" (*Letters* 157). Ultimately, in the year 1976 of the Third Age Isildur's descendant Aranarth takes "the title of Chieftain of the Dúnedain" and the heirlooms of the house of Isildur[8] "are given in keeping to Elrond" (*A* 334). The kingdom of Gondor further to the south endures long and even prospers, but eventually all of Anárion's[9] descendants die[10] and Gondor is ruled by a line of stewards. Then in TA 2463 the One Ring is found by Déagol, but Sméagol murders him and takes it (*FR* 59). Under its influence he gradually becomes Gollum and hides in the Misty Mountains, where the One Ring 'disappears' again: "The Ring went into the shadows with him, and even the maker, when his power had begun to grow again, could learn nothing of it" (*FR* 60). Sauron, at first, does not look for the Ring because "[h]e believed that the One had perished; that the Elves had destroyed it" (*FR* 58). In TA 2850, however, Gandalf finds out that Sauron is "seeking for news of the One, and of Isildur's Heir" (*A* 336).

While the ring is in Gollum's possession Aragorn is born in TA 2931. When he is "only two years old" his father is "slain by an orc-

---

8   The Ring of Barahir and the Sceptre of Annúminas. The shards of Narsil are already in Rivendell, taken there by Ohtar, Isildur's squire.
9   Anárion is Isildur's brother.
10 "The line of Meneldil son of Anárion failed, and the Tree withered, and the blood of the Númenoreans became mingled with that of lesser men" (*FR* 235).

arrow" (*A* 302). Aragorn is taken to Rivendell and "his true name and lineage were kept secret at the bidding of Elrond" (*A* 303). In TA 2939 Sauron's "servants are searching the Anduin near the Gladden Fields" (*A* 336), which indicates that he must have found out that the Ring was not destroyed. Two years later, when Aragorn is ten years old, the Ring comes into the possession of Bilbo and thus resurfaces. A year later Bilbo returns to the Shire and "Sauron returns in secret to Mordor" (*A* 337). Then, in TA 2951, Sauron "came to the dark tower and openly declared himself" (*FR* 240). This coincides with Aragorn's twentieth birthday. Although "only twenty years of age" Elrond saw that he

> was early come to manhood, though he would yet become greater in body and in mind. That day therefore Elrond called him by his true name, and told him who he was and whose son; and he delivered to him the heirlooms of his house. (*A* 303)

Note that Aragorn learns about his true identity at the moment that Sauron resumes power in Middle-earth. It echoes Gandalf's words:[11] "and that was in the very year of the finding of this Ring: a strange chance, if chance it was" (*FR* 240).

Aragorn does not see his inheritance as a burden. On the contrary, "his heart was high within him; and he sang, for he was full of hope and the world was fair" (*A* 303). It is in this moment that he first sees Arwen and falls in love. Elrond opposes their friendship, because he knows that the time will come when the Elves will leave Middle-earth and he wants to take Arwen with him. As both Elrond and Aragorn know that "many years of Men must still pass" (*A* 305), Aragorn leaves Rivendell to go out into the wild, where "[f]or nearly thirty years he laboured in the cause against Sauron; and he became a friend of Gandalf the Wise, from

---

[11] Spoken at the Council of Elrond where he tells how the White Council drove Sauron out of Mirkwood

whom he gained much wisdom" (*A* 305). Of his years in the wild Tolkien writes: "His ways were hard and long and he became somewhat grim to look upon, unless he chanced to smile; and yet he seemed to Men worthy of honour, as a king that is in exile, when he did not hide his true shape" (*A* 305).

When Aragorn is forty-nine he comes to Lothlórien. There he unexpectedly finds Arwen and she falls in love with him. They become betrothed and Aragorn gives her one of his heirlooms, the ring of Barahir.[12] When Elrond hears of the betrothal it saddens him and he informs Aragorn that Arwen "shall not be the bride of any Man less than the King of both Gondor and Arnor" (*A* 307).[13] The defeat of Sauron has now become doubly significant to Aragorn; he therefore renews his wanderings outside Rivendell. Meanwhile Arwen makes a great standard "such as only one might display who claimed the lordship of the Númenoreans and the inheritance of Elendil" (*A* 307). Then, in the year TA 3001, Bilbo holds his farewell party. Gandalf suspects that Bilbo's ring may be the One Ring, so he calls on Aragorn to find Gollum (*FR* 241). When the search seems in vain, Gandalf goes to Gondor to find out more about the One Ring. Meanwhile Aragorn has not abandoned his quest for Gollum and he eventually finds him. However, it is too late, Gollum has already been captured by Sauron and, under torture, he has revealed the name of the new owner of the Ring: the Ring plot is set in motion.[14] At the moment Sauron can still be beaten but when he regains the Ring he will be more powerful than before: "The Enemy still lacks one thing to give him strength and knowledge to beat down all resistance, break the

---

[12] Which is of extra significance because it once belonged to Beren, see note 13.

[13] In doing so he repeats the actions of King Thingol who set the mortal Beren the impossible task of recovering a Silmaril from the Crown of Morgoth before he would be permitted to wed Lúthien, Thingol's immortal elven daughter. She is Arwen's ancestor, with whom she is often compared.

[14] Although it takes another seventeen years before Frodo starts his journey.

last defences, and cover all the lands in a second darkness. He lacks the One Ring" (*FR* 57).

Not all of the above is known to the reader of *LOTR*. As we shall see Tolkien deliberately keeps hidden the true identity of Aragorn. Some information is given, but until the hobbits reach Rivendell it is sparse and easily overlooked. However, to adapt the character for other media, this information is indispensable because it shows Tolkien's view of Aragorn's role.

Tolkien's fondness of the Volsunga Saga, and especially the story of Sigurd, is well known.[15] And the similarities between their two life-stories are apparent. The fathers of both Aragorn and Sigurd are killed by an enemy. Sigurd's even before he is born.[16] In the saga Sigmund, with his dying breath, says to his wife Hjordis: "thou art great with a man-child; nourish him well; and with good heed, and the child shall be the noblest and most famed of all our kin" (Morris 1888, chapter XII).[17] Both Aragorn and Sigurd are the last of their line and both grow up in a sheltered environment. Aragorn's mother Gilraen finds a safe haven with Elrond. And Hjordis is taken in by King Hjalprek of Denmark. There Sigurd is fostered by Regin: "Now Sigurd's foster-father was hight Regin, the son of Hreidmar" (Morris 1888, chapter XIII); while Aragorn is fostered by Elrond: "Elrond took the place of his father and came to love him as a son of his own" (*A* 302-303). Both Aragorn and Sigurd have powerful non-human guardians. Sigurd has the Norse god Odin and

---

[15] Tolkien remarked about Andrew Lang's Sigurd story that "it was the best story that he had ever read" (Carpenter 2002:39). When Tolkien won the Skeat Prize for English in 1914 he spent five pounds of the prize money to buy Morris' translation of the *Volsunga Saga* and the related work *The House of the Wolfings* (Carpenter 2002:99).

[16] As some instances have already been quoted above, I will skip part of the Aragorn examples.

[17] I cannot give page numbers as I will quote from the online library version, but I will use chapter numbers instead.

Aragorn has Gandalf the Istari,[18] both of whom are portrayed as long-bearded old men.[19] Both Aragorn and Sigurd inherit a powerful sword. Sigurd inherits his father's sword Gram: "keep well withal the shards of the sword: thereof shall a goodly sword be made, and it shall be called Gram, and our son shall bear it, and shall work many a great work therewith" (Morris 1888, chapter XII). And Aragorn inherits Narsil, the sword of Isildur: "'Here is the ring of Barahir,' he [Elrond] said, 'the token of our kinship from afar;[20] and here also are the shards of Narsil'" (*A* 303). In both cases the swords have been broken in the battle that caused their last owner's death: "and as Sigmund smote fiercely with the sword it fell upon the bill and burst asunder in the midst" (Morris 1888, chapter XI). Before Sigurd and Aragorn can fight their first battle, the swords have to be forged anew: "So he [Regin] made a sword, and as he bore it forth from the forge, it seemed to the smiths as though fire burned along the edges thereof" (Morris 1888, chapter XV); "Very bright was that sword when it was made whole again; the light of the sun shone redly in it, and the light of the moon shone cold, and its edge was hard and keen" (*FR* 264). These similarities[21] – orphan, last of line, threat/sheltered, foster-father, non-human guardian, magical heirloom sword, and kingly destination – are not unique to Sigurd and Aragorn. They also appear in Arthurian, Carolingian and other legends. They follow the characteristic patterns of the hero myth as shown by Lord Raglan in his 1936 book *The Hero, a Study in Tradition, Myth and Drama*, by Joseph Campbell in his 1949 book *The Hero with a Thou-*

---

[18] Tolkien describes Gandalf as an "Odinic wanderer" (*Letters* 119).

[19] "an old man, long-bearded" (Morris 1888, chapter XIII); "An old man [...] He had a long white beard" (*FR* 32).

[20] The ring was used as a token by Barahir's son Beren when he sought Finrod's aid in the Quest of the Silmaril. Aragorn's line stems from Elros, Elrond's brother. Both are the sons of Eärendil the mariner who is a descendant of Beren and Lúthien.

[21] See also Day (2001:37-77), Day (2003:168-179), Jones (2002:72-74), Petty (2003:145, 164-166, 272), and Burdge and Burke (2004:154-156).

sand Faces, and by Georges Dumézil in his 1971 work *Mythe et Epopée II, Types épiques indo-européens: un héros, un sorcier, un roi*. They can also be found in Northrop Frye's (2000:186-206; first edition 1957) mythos of summer: the romance.

Tolkien did not deliberately create similarities with existing stories, he just recalled them: "always I had the sense of recording what was already 'there', somewhere: not of 'inventing'" (*Letters* 145). This does not mean, however, that his 'telling' of the events is not original:

> These tales are 'new', they are not directly derived from other myths and legends, but they must inevitably contain a large measure of ancient wide-spread motives or elements. After all I believe that legends and myths are largely made of 'truth', and indeed present aspects of it that can only be received in this mode; and long ago certain truths and modes of this kind were discovered and must always reappear. (*Letters* 147)

I agree with Houghton (2003), Shippey (2000 and 2003) and Chance (2004) who see Tolkien's stories as "the tendency of philologists to construct not only the forms of lost words (typically marked by a prefixed asterisk) and lost languages, but also the world-views that those words and languages described" (Houghton 2003:171), or as Shippey (2000:xv) puts it:

> However fanciful Tolkien's creation of Middle-earth was, he did not think that he was entirely making it up. He was 'reconstructing', he was harmonizing contradictions in his source-texts, sometimes he was supplying entirely new concepts (like hobbits), but he was also reaching back to an imaginative world which he believed had once really existed, at least in a collective imagination: and for this he had a very great deal of admittedly scattered evidence.

What Tolkien grasped was an inherent aspect of myth which Doniger calls the cross-cultural or transcultural experience:

> We often feel that various tellings of a much-retold myth are the same, at least in the sense that they do not disappoint us by omitting what we regard as essential parts of the myth, without which it would lose at the very least some of its charm, and at the most its meaning. When we say that two myths from two different cultures are 'the same' we mean that there are certain plots that come up again and again, revealing a set of human concerns that transcend any cultural barriers, experiences that we might call cross-cultural or transcultural. (Doniger 1998:53)

The transcultural aspect of myth makes it "an inherently comparative genre" (Doniger 1998:27), which Doniger does not limit to written media alone. But in order to compare a myth across different media it is necessary to first define the micromyth:

> The micromyth is the neutral structure [...] It is an imaginary text, a scholarly construct that contains the basic elements from which all the possible variants could be created, a theoretical construct that will enable us to look at all the variants at once and ask questions of all of them simultaneously.
> (Doniger 1998: 88)

As Doniger points out the micromyth is a scholarly construct necessary to reduce a story to its basic elements in order to make inter- and cross-media analysis possible. I have dubbed Aragorn's micromyth the hero-king myth. It can be summed up as follows:

- The hero (who can be male or female) is separated from his parents at an early age; in many hero-myths this is because one or both parents are slain by an enemy.

- The hero is fostered either in the normal chivalric tradition or because he is an orphan.
- The hero initially does not know his heritage or the destiny he has to fulfil.
- The hero has certain assets which make him stand out from other people.
- The hero distinguishes himself by his acts and deeds.
- The hero receives as heirloom an artefact with 'magical' properties (in West-European legends this usually is a sword).
- The hero has a non-human guardian.
- The kingdom suffers because of the absence of the rightful king.
- To become king the hero must prove that he is the true heir.

This list does not include another element common to both Aragorn's and Sigurd's stories, which shows that their myths are even more closely linked, namely Éowyn and Brynhild, respectively. Tolkien needs Éowyn for several reasons; the elemental being the creation of an asterisk-cosmogony.[22] On the one hand Éowyn is needed to kill the King of Angmar, the Lord of the Nazgûl of whom Gandalf says "if words spoken of old be true, not by the hand of man shall he fall" (*RK* 81).[23] On the other hand her healing by Aragorn through a kiss[24] echoes Brynhild's awakening by Sigurd and the kiss of the fairy prince that awakens Sleeping Beauty. The healing itself serves yet another purpose: to show that Aragorn is a true king.

Aragorn's similarities with Sigurd could be called the Germanic part of his character. They show Aragorn in the tradition of the Germanic or Celtic hero, but this is only one part of his character. Perhaps one could

---

[22] So termed by Houghton (2003) and Shippey (2003).
[23] Tolkien 'commenting' on the death of Macbeth.
[24] "he [Aragorn] bent and kissed her on the brow" (*RK* 127).

say that this is Aragorn in his *high mimetic* mode[25] (Frye 2000:34), Aragorn in his disguise as Ranger.[26] When his true lineage has been revealed to both Frodo and the council in Rivendell, his other role of King is shown more and more. This is Aragorn in the mode of *hero of romance*, the rightful heir to the kingdoms of Arnor and Gondor and the person who, through his rule, will bring peace and prosperity to Middle-earth. This transition is not as gradual or linear as presented here. It is closely tied in with the overall story. Aragorn's true identity must be hidden form Sauron until the time is ripe,[27] so his true lineage and appearance are mostly shown in places where it is safe to do so as in Rivendell or Lothlórien. Or when needed, for instance when Aragorn uses Athalas to treat Frodo's wound. Still, more and more elements of the *hero of romance* gradually come to light:

- Elven wisdom and the foresight of the Dúnedain.
- The power to heal (at first shown tentatively with Frodo, but when Aragorn 'has grown', in its full form when he seemingly recalls Éowyn from the dead).
- The sword-that-was-broken Narsil/Andúril of which it was foretold that is should be forged anew when the Ring was found (tied in with Boromir and Faramir's dream).
- Galadriel calls him Elessar, the name foretold as his royal name.
- Commanding the palantír of Orthanc.
- Commanding the Dead on the Paths of the Dead.
- Finding the sapling of the White Tree which grows and blossoms after he plants it in Gondor.

---

25 Although Frye's modes are presented as techniques of literary criticism they can also be used to compare other narrative media, especially when the original medium is text.

26 Note that the word Ranger is invariably spelled with a capital letter in *LOTR*.

27 I disagree with Øystein Høgset, who in his article 'The Adaptation of *The Lord of the Rings* – A Critical Comment' (2004) sees this transition as Aragorn "coming to terms with his heritage."

Tolkien very cleverly uses the other characters to show the transition from Ranger to king. When we read about Aragorn we must not forget that the larger part of *LOTR* is told from a hobbit's point of view.[28] What we mostly see, in their descriptions and comments, is Aragorn the Ranger, who even has another name: Strider. Bilbo, who knows more about Aragorn, calls him Dúnadan, leader of the Dúnedain, his Rivendell name. Bilbo is also the creator of the "All that is gold does not glitter"-verse (*FR* 238) that goes with the name of Aragorn (*FR* 170). It is obvious that Tolkien uses the verse not only to convince the hobbits that Aragorn is trustworthy, but also to alert us readers that we, too, should be aware that there is more to Aragorn than meets the eye.

Who then is this Strider, this Ranger? Tolkien first mentions Aragorn when Gandalf recounts the capture of Gollum to Frodo in the second chapter of the first book: "a friend: Aragorn, the greatest traveller and huntsman of this age" (*FR* 64). It should be noted that this is Gandalf speaking and his vision of Aragorn is different. He knows Aragorn's true lineage and what he and his Dúnedain have already done to oppose Sauron. Still it is not opportune for Tolkien to reveal this information at this early stage of the trilogy, so all we can deduce at the moment is that Aragorn is an exceptional Ranger.[29] It is in the common room of the Prancing Pony in Bree when we first encounter Aragorn.[30]

---

[28] "I have told the whole tale more or less through 'hobbits'" (*Letters* 246). As we shall see, this is part of Tolkien's scheme to keep Aragorn's identity hidden not only from Sauron, but also from the reader. This is also the reason why he suggested the title *The War of the Ring* for the last volume of *LOTR* when it had to be published, for economic reasons, as three volumes (*Letters* 167).

[29] A group of Men who "were taller and darker than the Men of Bree and were believed to have strange powers of sight and hearing, and to understand the languages of beasts and birds" (*FR* 149). This is, apart from the information that Rangers smoke pipe-weed, the first description given.

[30] I use the complete description because the first encounter with Aragorn will be the part that I will use for my comparison with the other versions.

> Suddenly Frodo noticed that a strange-looking weather-beaten man, sitting in the shadows near the wall, was also listening intently to the hobbit-talk. He had a tall tankard in front of him, and was smoking a long-stemmed pipe curiously carved. His legs were stretched out before him, showing high boots of supple leather that fitted him well, but had seen much wear and were now caked with mud. A travel-stained cloak of heavy dark-green cloth was drawn close about him, and in spite of the heat of the room he wore a hood that overshadowed his face; but the gleam of his eyes could be seen as he watched the hobbits.
>
> 'Who is that?' Frodo asked, when he got a chance to whisper to Mr. Butterbur. 'I don't think you introduced him?'
>
> 'Him?' said the landlord in an answering whisper, cocking an eye without turning his head. 'I don't rightly know. He is one of the wandering folk – Rangers we call them. [...] What his right name is I've never heard: but he's known round here as Strider. Goes about at a great pace on his long shanks; though he don't tell nobody what cause he has to hurry. [...]'
>
> Frodo found that Strider was now looking at him, as if he had heard or guessed all that had been said. Presently, with a wave of his hand and a nod, he invited Frodo to come over and sit by him. As Frodo drew near he threw back his hood, showing a shaggy head of dark hair flecked with grey, and in a pale stern face a pair of keen grey eyes.
>
> 'I am called Strider', he said in a low voice. 'I am very pleased to meet you.' (*FR* 155-156)

The visual description of Aragorn is as seen through Frodo's eyes; who and what he is, is Butterbur's interpretation. Still, Aragorn introduces himself as Strider.[31] As he explains later this is for his own protection: "I had to study *you* first, and make sure of you. The Enemy has set traps for me before now" (*FR* 169, italics in the original). In the meantime Frodo, the hobbits, and the reader encounter a grim looking man who knows about the Ring and who wants to join the company. Either the information he gives or his appearance convince Frodo that there is more to this man than meets the eye: "I think you are not really as you choose to look" (*FR* 164-165). However, even when Aragorn tells the hobbits his real name (already mentioned in Gandalf's letter that only Frodo, Sam and Pippin have read), we only get a glimpse of his real character: "He stood up, and seemed suddenly to grow taller. In his eyes gleamed a light, keen and commanding [...] his face softened by a sudden smile 'I am Aragorn son of Arathorn'" (*FR* 169-170). Tolkien uses this glimpse of Aragorn the king several times, for instance in Lórien where "those who saw him wondered; for they had not marked before how tall and kingly he stood, and it seemed to them that many years of toil had fallen from his shoulders" (*FR* 355), or when he answers Éomer's impertinent questions: "He seemed to have grown in stature while Éomer had shrunk; and in his living face they caught a brief vision of the power and majesty of the kings of stone" (*TT* 29). In Bree, however, we do not yet know the meaning of Bilbo's lines "Renewed shall be blade that was broken, [t]he crownless again shall be king" (*FR* 168). All we know is that the lines go with the name Aragorn, that Strider is Aragorn and that he possesses a broken sword of which he says: "the time is near when it shall be forged anew" (*FR* 170). Aragorn has, as yet, not been linked to the Dúnedain or to Isildur.

---

[31] In the next chapter Aragorn distances himself from the character Strider by speaking of Strider in the third person.

Tolkien shows us Aragorn's skills as a Ranger on the way to Rivendell. His knowledge of Athelas (the name Kingsfoil is not given) could well be part of these skills. Only after this episode, when Pippin asks him where he gets his knowledge from,[32] does Aragorn say that the "heirs of Elendil do not forget all things past" (*FR* 197). But this remark is so casual that Pippin overlooks it. Glorfindel calls Aragorn Dúnedan in his elven greeting but the hobbits do not notice this.[33] Only in the safe haven of Rivendell does Aragorn's ancestry become known. First Gandalf tells Frodo who Aragorn really is, to which Frodo responds: "'Do you really mean that Strider is one of the people of the old Kings? [...] I thought he was only a Ranger'" (*FR* 213). Finally, it is Elrond who informs those gathered at the council of Aragorn's true identity, after Boromir has recounted his and Faramir's dream:

> 'And here in the house of Elrond more shall be made clear to you' said Aragorn, standing up. He cast his sword upon the table that stood before Elrond, and the blade was in two pieces. 'Here is the Sword that was Broken!' he said.
> 'And who are you, and what have you to do with Minas Tirith?' asked Boromir, looking in wonder at the lean face of the Ranger and his weather-stained cloak.
> 'He is Aragorn son of Arathorn,' said Elrond; 'and he is descended through many fathers from Isildur

---

[32] Pippin adds that he cannot have learned it from the birds and beasts because "the birds and beasts do not tell tales of that sort" (*FR* 197), confirming that not only the Men of Bree believe that Rangers can talk to animals; another link between Aragorn and Sigurd.

[33] This becomes obvious in Rivendell when Bilbo waits for his friend Dúnedan and Frodo does not know that he means Aragorn. As Glorfindel is speaking Elvish, where the word *dún-adan* means Man of the West/Númenorean, only the reader knows that he is addressing Aragorn.

Elendil's son of Minas Ithil. He is the Chief of the Dúnedain in the North.' (*FR* 237)

At the council Gandalf tells the story of Aragorn's capture of Gollum a second time. But now that we know who he really is Tolkien cannot only reveal more, he can also show us how he sees Aragorn, as these are Aragorn's own words:

> 'There is little need to tell of them,' said Aragorn. 'If a man must needs walk in sight of the Black Gate, or tread the deadly flowers of Morgul Vale, then perils he will have. I, too, despaired at last, and I began my homeward journey. And then, by fortune, I came suddenly on what I sought: the marks of soft feet beside a muddy pool.' (*FR* 243)

Tolkien shows us a man who puts his own life at risk for a greater cause but does not boast about it. As Aragorn says himself "it seemed fit that Isildur's heir should labour to repair Isildur's fault" (*FR* 241). He admits fallibility by stating his despair and shows that finding Gollum was pure chance. So, although he is of high birth and chieftain of the Dúnedain, he undertakes the search and shows that he does not hold himself higher than other men.

Now the time to forge Narsil anew has also come. The Ring has been found and battle is at hand:

> Aragorn [...] turned to Boromir again. 'For my part I forgive your doubt,' he said. 'Little do I resemble the figures of Elendil and Isildur as they stand carven in their majesty in the halls of Denethor. I am but the heir of Isildur, not Isildur himself. I have had a hard life and a long [...] Our days have darkened, and we have dwindled; but ever the Sword has passed to a new keeper [...] But now the world is changing once again. A new hour comes. Isildur's Bane is found. Battle is at

> hand. The Sword shall be reforged. I will come to Minas Tirith.' (*FR* 238-239)

So before the Fellowship leaves Rivendell the sword is forged again. As Burdge and Burke (2004) point out, Narsil is a symbol of destiny. The broken sword motif is also part of many of the myths that belong to the hero-king cluster.[34] We must therefore assume that Aragorn carries Narsil for this reason, which seems to be exemplified when he unsheathes the sword in Bree after Bilbo's lines have been read out.[35] As Narsil can also identify him as Aragorn, the sword remains hidden at his side most of the time. However, he knows that the Ring is on its way to Rivendell, so presumably the main reason he has brought the sword is that it can be forged again, "for it was spoken of old among us that it should be made again when the Ring, Isildur's Bane, was found" (*FR* 237). At the moment, though, Aragorn's destiny does not lie with the Ring. As Elendil's heir he sees it as his duty to stand by Gondor:

> His own plan [...] had been to go with Boromir, and with his sword help to deliver Gondor. For he believed that the message of the dreams was a summons, and that the hour had come at last when the heir of Elendil should come forth and strive with Sauron for the mastery. (*FR* 349)

After the council Aragorn uses his full titles more often but always with prudence and only when he is sure that he is not addressing one of Sauron's henchmen. Although Elendil's heir must still remain hidden from Sauron's eyes, Tolkien can more and more stress the fact that this is Aragorn the king, not Strider the Ranger:

---

[34] As was already shown, it is also part of Sigurd's story, another hero-king myth.
[35] That Aragorn carries no other weapons save Narsil is shown when he has to defend the hobbits on the road to Rivendell: he uses flaming brands of wood.

> 'Fear not!' said a strange voice behind him. Frodo turned and saw Strider, and yet not Strider; for the weatherworn Ranger was no longer there. In the stern sat Aragorn son of Arathorn, proud and erect, guiding the boat with skilful strokes; his hood was cast back, and his dark hair was blowing in the wind, a light was in his eyes: a king returning from exile to his own land.
>
> 'Fear not!' he said. 'Long have I desired to look upon the likenesses of Isildur and Anárion, my sires of old. Under their shadow Elessar, the Elfstone son of Arathorn of the House of Valandil Isildur's son heir of Elendil, has nought to dread!' (FR 372)

These are the words of someone who is proud of his lineage and who is glad that the day is at hand when he can shed his disguise and fight Sauron openly. But it is only after the fall of Orthanc before the Battle of the Pelennor Fields that he can reveal his true identity to Sauron by using the palantír:

> 'It was a bitter struggle, and the weariness is slow to pass. I spoke no word to him, and in the end I wrenched the Stone to my own will. That alone he will find hard to endure. And he beheld me. [...] To know that I lived and walked the earth was a blow to his heart, I deem; for he knew it not till now. The eyes in Orthanc did not see through the armour of Théoden; but Sauron has not forgotten Isildur and the sword of Elendil. Now in the very hour of his great designs the heir of Isildur and the Sword are revealed; for I showed the blade re-forged to him. He is not so mighty yet that he is above fear; nay, doubt ever gnaws him.' (RK 46)

As we later learn he has done so to draw Sauron's attention to himself and away from Frodo. It is Gandalf's and Aragorn's intention that

Sauron should think that Isildur's heir shall claim the One Ring. However, now that the truth is revealed Tolkien can finally show Aragorn in his full mode of *hero of romance* and it is only after this moment that the major points of this mode, namely the Paths of the Dead, the houses of Healing and the finding of the sapling of the White Tree are told. Aragorn now also displays the banner that Arwen made:

> [U]pon the foremost ship a great standard broke, and the wind displayed it as she turned towards the Harlond. There flowered a White Tree, and that was for Gondor; but Seven Stars were about it, and a high crown above it, the signs of Elendil that no lord had borne for years beyond count. And the stars flamed in the sunlight, for they were wrought of gems by Arwen daughter of Elrond; and the crown was bright in the morning, for it was wrought of mithril and gold.
>
> Thus came Aragorn son of Arathorn, Elessar, Isildur's heir, out of the Paths of the Dead, borne upon a wind from the Sea to the kingdom of Gondor.
> (*RK* 108-109)

But Aragorn does not claim his kingship even after the battle has been won. At the last debate he says: "I do not yet claim to command any man" (*RK* 139). It is Imrahil, Prince of Dol Amroth, who first acknowledges Aragorn's new role: "'As for me,' said Imrahil, 'the Lord Aragorn I hold to be my liege lord, whether he claims it or no'" (*RK* 139). And later, when they ride out towards the Black Gate in a last attempt to gain more time for Frodo, it is again Imrahil who says: "'Say not *The Lords of Gondor*. Say *The King Elessar*. For that is true, even though he has not yet sat upon the throne'" (*RK* 143, italics in the original). Aragorn's final transition comes after the Ring is destroyed, when Elrond arrives with the sceptre of Annúminas and with Arwen, keeping his promise that Arwen may wed Aragorn when he has shown that he is the true heir of Elendil:

> [A]nd last came Master Elrond, mighty among Elves and Men, bearing the sceptre of Annúminas, and beside him upon a grey palfrey rode Arwen his daughter, Evenstar of her people.
>   And Frodo [...] said to Gandalf: 'At last I understand why we have waited! This is the ending.'
> (*RK* 221)

Is it possible to translate Aragorn's complex transition to another medium? And, if not, is this because of the medium's restrictions or of the mediator's choices?

RALPH BAKSHI'S ARAGORN

The problem with any adaptation of *LOTR* is that the story has to be condensed. Choices have to be made and Tolkien himself was well aware of this: "an *abridgement* by selection with some good picture work would be pleasant" (*Letters* 261). Another problem, especially with the character of Aragorn, is his duality of both Ranger and king: the man we get to see in Bree has to incorporate both the grim, sinewy and at times gaunt looking Ranger and the stature and nobility of the future king. Another complication, as with any text, is that the reader forms his/her own mental pictures and, to add to this, *LOTR* is a thoroughly visual work, so anyone attempting to put the words into images will always displease someone. Cross media content analysis should also take into account that each medium has its own apparatus to convey a narrative to its audience. This not only implies that audience expectations are media specific, but also that every adaptation is the product of at least three modifications: the choices made by the person or persons creating the adaptation, the 'language' of the medium used, and the restrictions posed by the medium. When examining the different versions of the Bree scene, I will therefore very briefly sum up the major restrictions of the medium used and the main means by which it depicts character.[36]

The first film adaptation of *LOTR* is Ralph Bakshi's animated film version made in 1978. The most obvious restriction posed by the medium is of course length. In an attempt to address this problem Bakshi planned to make two films. The 1978 picture is the only one produced and it ends after the battle at Helm's Deep. A film evidently tells a story through visualization and the angle, level, height, distance and other qualities of framing strongly influence the way we view a character.[37] Bakshi combines traditional cell animation with rotoscoped live-action footage to tell his version. However Bakshi prefers "old fashioned animation"[38] for character animation which, depending on the animation style used, usually means that facial features and expressions are less distinct.

As with Tolkien's version we first see Aragorn in the common room of the inn at Bree, in a close-up[39] of Frodo who looks round to assess the other guests at the inn. As the camera pans round we see Strider sitting in the background. When Frodo looks away from Strider we get a medium long shot of Aragorn as Strider. We see a man sitting comfortably with his back against the wall and his legs stretched out before him, smoking a long plain pipe. He is wearing beige coloured boots, a brown coloured short-sleeved tunic with a large belt and a disproportionably large belt buckle. His eyes are hidden by the hood of the long dark-brown mantle that he is wearing. Around his wrists we see leather

---

[36] It is impossible to do this adequately within the scope of this article. The reader should only take it as a reminder that the media used are very diverse.

[37] As Bordwell and Thompson (2001:220) point out the context of the film ultimately determines the function of the framings; so one should be careful when attributing meaning to framing techniques.

[38] Bakshi in an interview by Patrick Naugle in 2004.

[39] A close up of a character usually only shows the head, hands or feet; the medium close shot shows the body from the chest up; the medium shot from the waist and the medium long shot from the knees or completely.

arm cuffs and his left arm rests on the pommel of a clearly visible sword at his left side. His legs are bare, and his skin tone is much darker than that of the hobbits. Contrary to Tolkien's description, his clothes do not look muddy or worn and Narsil, though sheathed, is clearly visible.[40] Frodo does not ask Butterbur who the man is. In the next shots we sometimes see Strider in the background of the frame, always in the same pose. He only looks up once when Frodo is singing his song.

After Frodo's debacle with the Ring the hobbits flee to their room where Strider is already waiting. As he stands up we see that he wears a brown band above the elbow of his left arm and that his hair is black and comes to the nape of his neck. His face is clean-shaven and looks grim but not gaunt. It is dominated by a crooked nose with a clearly visible hook. His eyes are black. His somewhat broad face with the crooked nose and his broad shoulders make him look more like a wrestler than a ragged man used to living in the wild. He certainly does not match Tolkien's description in Gandalf's letter:[41] "a Man, lean, dark, tall." As he has not been introduced, he tells the hobbits that his name is Strider and that he is a friend of Gandalf's. In Bakshi's version, Gandalf's letter is omitted so that Strider's rebuke of Butterbur "there is no one else for them to take up with except a fat innkeeper who only remembers his name because people shout it at him all day", seems more cruel and even arrogant. In the original text Aragorn uses almost the same words but there he speaks in anger because if Butterbur had not forgotten the letter, Frodo and the Ring would have been safe at Rivendell before the riders had found the Shire; so even his words make Bakshi's Aragorn less noble than the Ranger Tolkien shows us. The following action seems to confirm this because when Sam challenges him shortly after Butterbur has left, Aragorn says: "if I wanted the Ring for myself, I could have it,

---

[40] Compare the original "a sword that had hung concealed by his side" (*FR* 169).
[41] As I have hopefully shown before, Gandalf's depiction of Aragorn is more reliable and is probably the way Tolkien would describe him himself.

now;" and then draws his sword. The hobbits cower back until they see that a third of the sword is missing, including the point. Then Aragorn says: "My name is Aragorn, son of Arathorn. If by life or death I can safe you, I will." And the scene ends.

As the viewers do not know Bilbo's rhymes, this name does not mean anything. Until this moment it has not been mentioned, and although he knows Frodo's real name and why the riders follow him, compared to the original there is nothing to corroborate this. Frodo seems to rely only on his intuition when he says "I think one of the enemy's servants would, well, seem fairer and feel fouler" to convince Sam that Strider can be trusted. In the original Frodo uses these words to explain to Aragorn that he wanted to believe him before Gandalf's letter came. However, the least credible element in Bakshi's version of Aragorn is Narsil. As Tolkien puts it himself "Strider does not 'Whip out a sword' in the book. Naturally not: his sword was broken" (*Letters* 273). And this is exactly what this Aragorn does: he whips out his sword, where in the original he only lays his hand on the hilt, but does not draw the sword at this moment. Narsil is only unsheathed to show the hobbits that Aragorn carries the broken sword as mentioned in Bilbo's poem. The usual reaction of my students to this scene is laughter as Aragorn looks completely ridiculous. This is enhanced by the camera angle which attempts to show Aragorn from a hobbit's point of view. Furthermore Narsil is broken at the wrong end. Narsil is "broken a foot below the hilt" (*FR* 170), not a foot above the tip. Anyway, without the rhyme or Aragorn's words about the re-forging of the sword, what good is this broken sword? Only those who have read the book prior to seeing the film know who Aragorn and Narsil are. And although Bakshi's adaptation certainly tries to be true to the book within the limitations given, because of the choices made only fans of the books know this. The depiction of Aragorn is that of a Ranger as envisioned by Bakshi. The way he looks and behaves not only makes him implausible as a future king but even reduces his mimetic mode to that of *low* or even *ironic mimesis*. And although he shows Narsil, without the proper context we cannot place him in the hero-king tradition.

SIBLEY AND BAKEWELL'S ARAGORN

In a radio play, character is mainly shown through the voice of the actor who "represents his feeling for the character in tone and style" (*Letters* 254). And although the medium is not as restrictive as film where the length of the adaptation is concerned, Tolkien's main reason for deeming *LOTR* unsuitable for dramatization is because "it needs more space, a lot of space" (*Letters* 255). Dramatization also means that the original text, including descriptions of the scenery, has to be transformed into dialogue. Only actions that can be made audible, like running feet, slamming doors, rustling paper, can be 'translated'. As this is characteristic of the medium, audiences expect these 'aural' props.

In the 1981 BBC radio play by Brian Sibley and Michael Bakewell, Aragorn is introduced in the following scene:

> [Common room of the inn, voices mumbling in the background]
> *Frodo*: Mister Butterbur who's that strange-looking weather-beaten man sitting by the wall smoking a pipe? I don't think you introduced him.
> *Butterbur*: Oh him. I don't rightly know. He is one of the wandering folk – Rangers we call 'em. He disappears for a month, or a year, and then he pops up again. What his right name is I've never heard: but he's known round here as Strider.
> *Frodo*: Why's that?
> *Butterbur*: Well on account of his going about at a great pace on his long shanks of his [Frodo laughs] though he don't tell nobody what cause he has to hurry.

This dialogue is very close to the original. The encounter with Strider even lasts almost as long, so that all the essential parts, including the long conversation before Gandalf's letter and the letter itself, are included. There is a slight difference though. Gandalf's letter is read aloud so that all present, including Strider, hear the contents. In the original, Aragorn speaks the first lines of the rhyme as a response to Frodo's description of his looks, thus unwittingly confirming that he is the real Strider, as Frodo shows by his question "Did the verses apply to you then? [...] But how did you know that they were in Gandalf's letter, if you have never seen it?" (*FR* 170). Narsil then is only secondary proof that he is who he claims to be. In the radio play, Narsil becomes the sole proof of his true identity and therefore gains in importance. This is enhanced by the fact that the verses are accompanied by dramatic music, making them sound more like a prophesy than verses of a hobbit friend.

The most crucial element of this adaptation is, of course, the actor who provides Aragorn's voice. As Brian Sibley (1995:12) says himself in the accompanying booklet, Robert Stephens was a controversial decision: "He was, for some, an unlikely choice; but for a great many listeners Robert's powerfully idiosyncratic performance embodied a strong sense of Aragorn's lost nobility." Sibley does not elaborate, so I can only speculate that the choice was controversial because Stephens was mostly known for his many Shakespearian roles and recordings. My Dutch students are not aware of this; they describe the voice as being wise, older and trustworthy, elements of *high mimesis*. The listener's comments thus show that this Aragorn is a believable future king. The iconic use of Narsil not only shows Aragorn as a *hero of romance*, it also roots this version firmly in the hero-king tradition.

PETER JACKSON'S ARAGORN

Peter Jackson's live-action version solves the problem of length by making three films, each lasting approximately three hours, the extended DVD versions even lasting up to forty-eight minutes longer. As has been noted earlier, Jackson's version is action oriented and to pace the tempo, the films are divided up differently from the books. Because each film had to stand on its own, new scenes were added either to maintain balance or to provide necessary information. However, in doing so they deviate dramatically from the original and the film ceases to be an adaptation.[42] The great strength of Jackson's version is the visualization. It is not surprising therefore that, as far as outer appearance is concerned, this Aragorn hits the mark. As Jackson says in the commentary: "like the description of Tolkien's, of Strider sitting in a corner of the room and it is great to be able to just like nail them on screen." (FELLOWSHIP OF THE RING EXTENDED DVD VERSION)

Apart from his pipe, which is not "curiously carved" (*FR* 155), this is Aragorn as Frodo sees him, including the boots "caked with mud" (*ibid*) and the "travel-stained cloak" (*ibid*). His gaunt looking face, unshaven beard and greasy hair show us a man who has long been on the road, a true Ranger. This depiction of Aragorn has only one major 'fault'; he is wearing the ring of Barahir. As we shall later see, Aragorn is not carrying Narsil, so the ring has, at some time in the future but not in Bree, to serve as proof of his identity.[43]

---

[42] Peter Jackson, Fran Welsh and Philippa Boyens in the commentary (LORD OF THE RINGS: THE TWO TOWERS, EXTENDED DVD VERSION) give at least four different reasons why Aragorn goes over the cliff; well aware that they have overstepped the boundaries.

[43] The ring's name is only given in the extended version of THE TWO TOWERS. Until that moment only the true Tolkien fan can identify the ring by the way it looks. But the true Tolkien fan also knows that the ring was given to Arwen. See the beginning of this article and notes 12 and 13.

As the Bree scene lasts about three minutes (excluding Frodo's putting on the Ring) I will give the complete dialogue here:

> [Sam and Frodo are eating at a table in the common room of the Prancing Pony]
> *Sam*: That fellow's done nothing but stare at you [close up of Frodo] since we arrived. [Frodo takes a furtive look, camera shows a long shot of Aragorn sitting in the corner, followed by a medium to long shot of the Hobbits at the table.]
> *Frodo* [to Butterbur]: Excuse me. That Man in the corner who is he?
> *Butterbur* [close up]: He's one of them Rangers. [close up of Frodo and Sam] They're dangerous folk [long shot of Strider], wandering the Wilds. [camera zooms in to medium close shot] What his right name is I've never heard, [close up of Butterbur] but around here he is known as Strider.
> [Extreme close up of Strider's pipe and eyes. Back to Frodo who feels compelled to put on the Ring, but comes to his senses just in time when he hears Pippin mention the name Baggins. In his rush (medium close shot of Strider taking his pipe out of his mouth) to reach Pippin he falls (medium close shot of Strider sitting up) and the Ring slips on his finger. Ring sequence. When Frodo is visible again Strider's hand grabs him and pulls him away. Close up of Frodo.]
> *Strider* [hooded]: You draw far [close up of Strider] too much attention to yourself [Strider takes Frodo by the shoulder] "Mr. Underhill."
> [Strider shoves Frodo up some stairs and into the back room.]
> *Frodo* [close up]: What do you want?
> [The hooded Strider, while talking, walks over to the candles that illuminate the room.]

Strider [close up]: A little more caution from you; that is no trinket you carry.
Frodo [close up]: I carry nothing.
Strider [medium close shot, extinguishes candles]: Indeed. I can avoid being seen if I wish ... [candles are out] but to disappear entirely [Strider pulls away his hood] that is a rare gift.
Frodo [close up]: Who are you?
Strider [close up]: Are you frightened?
Frodo: Yes.
Strider [close up]: Not nearly frightened enough. I know what hunts you. [Starts walking towards Frodo; medium close shot of Strider turning while drawing his sword (which is not broken). The door opens and the other Hobbits burst in]
Sam [medium close shot]: Let him go! Or I'll have you Longshanks.
Strider [medium close shot]: You have a stout heart, little Hobbit. [Sheaths his sword, shot turns back to Sam, Merry and Pippin.] But that will not save you. [close up of Frodo] You can no longer wait for [close up of Aragorn] the wizard, Frodo. They're coming.

In Jackson's version nothing Strider does or says justifies the hobbits trusting him. What he tells Frodo could also have been used to lure the hobbits into a false sense of security. Only on the road to Rivendell does Merry ask "How do we know that this Strider is a friend of Gandalf's?" We must assume, though we have not seen it,[44] that more information was given at Bree. Frodo answers Merry's question with "I think a servant of the enemy would look fairer but feel fouler" and somewhat fatalistically adds "We have no choice but to trust him." So eventually,

---

[44] Not even in the extended DVD version.

as in the book, it is Frodo's intuition that makes him follow Strider. In the Bree scene Jackson does not use Narsil because:

> The one thing that I knew from the book that I could never do in the movie, mainly because I could never imagine it working, was the rather iconic moment where Strider pulls out his sword and it's the broken sword. And I just thought, 'Well, it's great in a book but in a movie people are going to laugh. This heroic figure pulls out the sword and there's only half a sword in his scabbard because half of it has broken off.' I just thought it's gonna get a laugh. Especially for people that don't know the books.
> (director's commentary FELLOWSHIP OF THE RING EXTENDED DVD VERSION)

Without Narsil Bilbo's verses are superfluous. In fact, Jackson's version is the only one that completely leaves out the letter; no doubt because it would slow down the fast paced action of the scene.

Similar to Tolkien's version we only find out Aragorn's true identity at the council of Elrond. But the primary reason is not that Aragorn's real identity has to remain hidden from Sauron, it is because Aragorn fears that he will make the same mistake Isildur has made. This Aragorn is not proud of his heritage, so in the Jackson films the transition from Ranger to king is the reluctant struggle of an heir who doubts his bloodline and his part in the Ring quest. In doing so, Jackson turns the Germanic hero into a renaissance Hamlet full of doubt and fallibility. By leaving out Narsil there is nothing that identifies this Aragorn with a *hero of romance*. His actions at Bree do not even show him in a *high mimetic* mode. And because Jackson recasts his role to that of the reluctant heir, most of the elements of the hero-king myth are also omitted from the story. In doing so Jackson shows Aragorn as a modern type action hero, giving the present generation of movie goers a hero they can identify with.[45]

COMPUTER GAMER'S ARAGORN

My final comparison will look at the official *FELLOWSHIP OF THE RING* game produced by Vivendi. I chose this game because, contrary to most other recent *LOTR* games, it is not based on the Peter Jackson films[46] but on Tolkien's book. Computer game adaptations of books or films differ from other media in that they give the player the opportunity to actively participate in the story by playing one of the characters. In the Vivendi game the player first takes on the role of Frodo, but when action demands it, he switches to Aragorn and later on also to Gandalf. To create a computer game, the greater part of *FR* is translated into action. In the beginning of the game, for instance, the player has to search Frodo's house to find the Ring. As this could result in a totally different story, player action is interrupted from time to time by non-interactive cut-scenes to advance the story. Truly great games make the interactive sequences so immersive that the player 'feels' part of the story and thus gets a better understanding of the ordeal the characters have to undergo. The time spent playing a computer game is usually not a reflection of the actual story time but of the time it takes the player to overcome the game's obstacles and puzzles. Fortunately, in the *FELLOWSHIP OF THE RING* these obstacles and puzzles are all linked to the original story.[47]

---

[45] A non-representative survey I held amongst first and second year students showed that most of them see Aragorn as the true hero of the films.

[46] The film-based games are all action orientated. In the PlayStation 2, Gamecube and X-Box version of the *TWO TOWERS*, the player can only take on the role of Aragorn, Legolas or Gimli. In *THE RETURN OF THE KING* Gandalf, Sam and Frodo are also playable characters. In both Game Boy Advanced versions the player can choose between all of these and even play as Éowyn. In these games the action required clearly depends on the character chosen; this makes them more interesting.

[47] As we shall see a bit later on 'linked to' not necessarily means that these events happened in the original.

Story and character visualization are usually done through animation, although part of the appeal of the film-based games comes from the transitions between the interactive animated sequences and the live-action cut-scenes taken from the films. Visual detail in computer games largely depends on the graphic capabilities of the computer platform for which the game has been produced. As a rule, cut-scenes, which are all pre-recorded, show greater detail than the interactive parts, which are visualized while the game is being played.

Because the Bree scene is a vital part of the story it is shown in an animated cut-scene. When you enter the inn, as Frodo, there is no one behind the counter. You have to walk on into the common room where the other hobbits already are. Apart from a dwarf you see some very unsavoury characters, one of which appears to be Bill Ferny. Contrary to the book, Strider is standing. He is a tall man, who fits Gandalf's description of lean, dark and tall. His square jaw bears the shadow of a beard and his face looks serious.[48] He has prominent cheekbones, dark eyebrows, dark eyes, and his long sleek dark hair comes well below his shoulders. He is not dressed like Tolkien's Aragorn, and does not wear a cloak – presumably because that would be inconvenient for the ensuing fight sequences. This is also the reason why he carries a bow and a quiver of arrows; and why he carries a functioning sword instead of Narsil. He is wearing a padded doublet with a long-sleeved shirt underneath, period buckskin hoses and long boots. His hands are covered by long gloves that also cover his lower arms. As decoration he wears a small shield-like device with the design of a cross on his chest. None of his clothing seems to be stained or torn, but this can be due to lack of detail. For a Ranger he is appropriately dressed. However, from his clothes and the weapons he carries it is immediately clear that this Aragorn has been 'designed' to play a more active role in the game.

---

[48] Alec Baldwin comes to mind.

When you walk up to him he greets you cordially and although you introduce yourself as Mr. Underhill, he does not give his own name. To advance the game Strider instructs you to get a room. So you walk back to the counter where Butterbur has arrived. His lines are very similar to those in the book. After this cut-scene you have to walk back to the common room for the main Bree scene:

> [As soon as you enter the room, the cut-scene starts with Pippin telling the other guests about Bilbo's birthday party. Frodo walks over to Strider]
> *Strider*: Master Underhill I'd stop your friend from talking if I was you. [Pippin goes on, coming to the part about the Ring] You'd better do something quick. [Song-ring sequence. Frodo reappears]
> *Strider*: What you did was worse than anything your friend could have said.
> *Frodo*: It was an accident.
> *Strider*: I want a word with you somewhere quiet.
> [Cut to the hobbits' room, Strider seems to be getting up from the stone ledge of the hearth. The camera shows him from a low angle, to represent hobbit eye-level. When the camera focuses on the hobbits the shot is shown from a high angle, to represent Strider's eye-level. Unlike Bakshi's film, these camera positions work and they give the scene more atmosphere.]
> *Sam*: Hello. Who are you? And what do you want?
> *Strider*: I am called Strider. And if what I say is helpful to you, I want you to take me with you.
> *Frodo*: I would not agree to any such thing till I knew a lot more about you.
> *Strider*: Excellent. You seem to be coming to your senses again after your accident ...
> *Butterbur*: [enters the room] Beggin' your pardon. I need a word.

Sam: Everyone in this place needs a word.
Butterbur: I remembered what it was I forgot.
Frodo: What?
Butterbur: About a Shire Hobbit named Baggins, but called Underhill.
Frodo: Who told you this?
Butterbur: Gandalf the wizard. He asked me to send this letter to you in the Shire. But I forgot. I, I expect he will turn me into a block of wood.
[Frodo reads the letter silently, we hear Gandalf's voice]
Gandalf: Dear Frodo, bad news. You must leave for Rivendell before the end of July. Do not wait for your birthday. I will meet you if I can, or follow you if I can't.
Frodo [reads on, presumably to himself, but his lips are moving]: You can trust the ranger called Strider. But make sure he is the real Strider. His true name is Aragorn [turns to look at Strider].
Strider: I am Aragorn, son of Arathorn. And if by life or death I can safe you, I will. I thought I would have to persuade you without proof, but my looks are against me.
Frodo: I believed you, or I wanted to. The enemy spies look fair but feel foul. While you feel fair ...
Strider: But look foul. [Sam laughs]
Pippin: Hold on, where is Merry? He is still not back from his walk.
Strider: Stay here. I'll find him.

Compared to Bakshi's and Jackson's versions more lines and elements of the original are kept. This holds true for all the lengthy cut-scenes in the game.[49] In Gandalf's letter Bilbo's verses have been left out, probably

---

[49] Confirming that this is the official game sanctioned by the Tolkien Estate.

because they do not make any sense without Narsil. And since this Aragorn will have to fight to fulfil his role as game warrior, he cannot carry Narsil with him. So in this version Gandalf's letter serves as sole proof that he is Aragorn, and as he reacts to the letter, Frodo must have read the last part loud enough for Aragorn to hear. When the game commences it becomes clear that, more than the Aragorn of the book, this Aragorn has to fulfil the part of the warrior in the game,[50] which primarily asks for fighting skills with sword and bow. This becomes immediately clear from the interactive part that follows where Aragorn, in an obvious change from the book, goes out to save Merry. To do this he, assisted by the other hobbits, has to fight and kill the unsavoury characters first seen in the common room, including Bill Ferny, who accuses him of wanting to keep the reward for finding the hobbits to himself. After Bree, on route to Rivendell, Aragorn has to face orcs, wargs and even trolls, where in the book there are none. The fights often take place in broad daylight whereas Tolkien emphasised that minions of the Enemy mostly fight in the dark and that light and fire can be used effectively to drive them off.

In short, in the interactive parts he is not Tolkien's Aragorn, he is an action based game warrior. And this is the duality shown in the game. Not that of Ranger versus king but that of cut-scene book Aragorn versus interactive game warrior, where the warrior tilts the balance. The part of game warrior has no need for the elements of the hero of *high romance* nor of any elements of the hero-king myth. After Rivendell Andúril becomes part of Aragorn's inventory, but not so much as a proof of his kingship, but as the superior melee weapon needed for future battle.

---

[50] Fantasy type games have typical roles a character can assume; the most common being warrior, magic user, and thief. These roles ultimately go back to Tolkien's *LOTR* (see Veugen 2004:94), so that we now have the situation that a character is acting out a role the original character helped to create.

CONCLUSION

Peter Jackson's interpretation of Tolkien's book has shifted the audience attention to the character of Aragorn and for those who have seen his trilogy, Viggo Mortensen will always be Aragorn. As Strider he – at least visually (apart from his weapons) – looks the part. Yet Jackson presents us at the same time an Aragorn that is very different from the one Tolkien envisioned. To set the balance right I have tried to show the real Aragorn as he is portrayed in *LOTR*, including the appendices and Tolkien's letters. I have used Wendy Doniger's micromyth and Northrop Frye's fictional modes to find those elements that define Aragorn's duality. I then looked at several adaptations of the first encounter with Aragorn in Bree, to see whether and how this duality was presented in other media, bearing in mind the principal characteristics of each medium. However, as I have found in my lectures, although some of the other interpretations are perhaps more true to the original, Jackson's vision dominates even when the original text has been read for reference. It seems that, for the time being at least, Jackson's Aragorn is the new standard. Still, every generation has adapted *LOTR* to suit its own needs; this is part of the book's strength and lasting appeal. And, in my view at least, also due to Tolkien's use of "ancient wide-spread motives [and] elements" (*Letters* 147).

CONNIE VEUGEN studied English language and literature at the Vrije Universiteit in Amsterdam. Her studies included Old and Middle English and Old Norse, subjects she took as a direct result of reading *The Lord of the Rings*. She currently works as a lecturer at the Vrije Universiteit Faculty of Arts' Comparative Art Studies, specializing in Culture and Digital Media. Her current research focuses on narrative, affect and immersion in computer games and cross- and inter-media comparison of computer games with other media. Her latest article 'Here be Dragons' (2004) deals with the pre-history, birth and early history of adventure games and Tolkien's role in the process.

References

Primary Sources

BASKHI, Ralph (director), 1978, J.R.R. TOLKIEN THE LORD OF THE RINGS, DVD version, Warner Home Video.

BLACK LABEL GAMES (production), 2002, *THE LORD OF THE RINGS: THE FELLOWSHIP OF THE RING PC GAME*, Vivendi International Games.

JACKSON, Peter (director), 2000, THE LORD OF THE RINGS: THE FELLOWSHIP OF THE RING, New Line Cinema.

JACKSON, Peter (director), 2001, THE LORD OF THE RINGS: THE FELLOWSHIP OF THE RING EXTENDED DVD VERSION, New Line Cinema.

JACKSON, Peter (director), 2003, THE LORD OF THE RINGS: THE TWO TOWERS EXTENDED DVD VERSION, New Line Cinema.

MORRIS, William, 1888, *The Story Of The Volsungs with Excerpts from the Poetic Edda*, Online Medieval and Classical Library Release #29, http://sunsite.berkeley.edu/OMACL/Volsunga/ [feb. 2005]

SIBLEY Brian and Michael BAKEWELL (dramatizers), 1995, *The Lord of the Rings Radio Play* [1987], BBC Worldwide Ltd.

TOLKIEN, J.R.R., 1974, *The Fellowship of the Ring* [1954], London: Unwin Books.

TOLKIEN, J.R.R., 1974, *The Two Towers* [1954], London: Unwin Books.

TOLKIEN, J.R.R., 1974, *The Return of the King* [1955], London: Unwin Books.

Secondary Sources

BORDWELL, David and Kristin THOMPSON, 2001, *Film Art: an Introduction*, (sixth edition, first edition 1979), New York: McGraw-Hill.

BURDGE, Anthony S. and Jessica BURKE, 2004, 'Humiliated Heroes: Peter Jackson's Interpretation of *The Lord of the Rings*', in Thomas HONEGGER (ed.), 2004, *Translating Tolkien: Text and Film*, Zurich and Berne: Walking Tree Publishers, pp. 135-164.

CAMPBELL, Joseph, 1973, *The Hero with a Thousand Faces*, (first edition 1949), Princeton: Princeton University Press.

CARPENTER, Humprey (ed.), 2000, *The Letters of J.R.R. Tolkien* (first edition 1981), New York: Houghton Mifflin.

CARPENTER, Humprey, 2002, *J.R.R. Tolkien: a Biography*, (first edition 1977), London: HarperCollins.

CHANCE, Jane (ed.), 2003, *Tolkien the Medievalist*, New York: Routledge.

CHANCE, Jane (ed.), 2004, *Tolkien and the Invention of Myth*, Lexington: University Press of Kentucky.

DAY, David, 2001, *Tolkien's Ring*, (first edition 1994), New York: Friedman/Fairfax Publishers.

DAY, David, 2003, *The World of Tolkien: Mythological Sources of The Lord of the Rings*, London: Mitchell Beazley.

DONIGER, Wendy, 1998, *The Implied Spider: Politics & Theology in Myth*, New York: Columbia University Press.

DUMEZIL, Georges, 1971, *Mythe et Epopée II, Types épiques indo-européens: un héros, un sorcier, un roi*. Paris: Gallimard.

FRYE, Northrop, 2000, *Anatomy of Criticism*, (first edition 1957), Princeton: Princeton University Press.

HØGSET, Øystein, 2004, 'The Adaptation of *The Lord of the Rings* – A Critical Comment', in Thomas HONEGGER (ed.), 2004, *Translating Tolkien: Text and Film*, Zurich and Berne: Walking Tree Publishers, pp. 165-180.

HONEGGER, Thomas (ed.), 2004, *Translating Tolkien: Text and Film*, Zurich and Berne: Walking Tree Publishers.

HOUGHTON, John William, 2003, 'Augustine in the Cottage of Lost Play: the *Ainulindalë* as Asterisk Cosmogony', in Jane CHANCE (ed.), 2003, *Tolkien the Medievalist*, New York: Routledge, pp. 171-182.

JONES, Leslie Ellen, 2002, *Myth & Middle-earth: Exploring the Legends behind J.R.R. Tolkien's The Hobbit & The Lord of the Rings*, New York: Cold Spring Press.

LORD RAGLAN, 2003, *The Hero: A Study in Tradition, Myth and Drama*, (first published 1936), New York: Dover Publications.

NAUGLE, Patrick, 2004, *Rotoscoped Memories: An Interview with Ralph Bakshi*, http://www.dvdverdict.com/specials/ralphbakshi.php [Febr. 2005]

PETTY, Anne C., 2003, *Tolkien in the Land of Heroes: Discovering the Human Spirit*, New York: Cold Spring Press.

SHIPPEY, Tom, 2000, *J.R.R. Tolkien: Author of the Century*, New York: Houghton Mifflin.

SHIPPEY, Tom, 2003, *The Road to Middle-earth: How J.R.R. Tolkien Created a New Mythology*, (3rd edition, first edition 1982), New York: Houghton Mifflin.

VEUGEN, Connie, 2004, 'Here be Dragons: voorgeschiedenis en ontstaan van adventure games', in *Tijdschrift voor Mediageschiedenis* 7/2004, pp. 77-99.

The Swiss Tolkien Society *EREDAIN*

The Swiss Tolkien Society *EREDAIN* was founded in 1986. Our main aims are to further the study of and the interest in the life and work of late Prof. J.R.R. Tolkien and contribute to the enjoyment of his creation, Middle-earth, in Switzerland.

Our society hosts a monthly discussion group and organises other Tolkien- and fantasy related events such as Middle-earth quizzes, readings, visits to Medieval markets etc. In addition, the society issues a fanzine named *Aglared* once a year. The members of *EREDAIN* share the pleasure in Tolkien's creation with our sister societies in many countries near and far.

If you are interested in our activities, please visit our website at:
> www.eredain.ch

or contact us via:
> kontakt@eredain.ch

or by mail:
> Swiss Tolkien Society
> P.O. Box 1916
> CH-8021 Zurich
> Switzerland

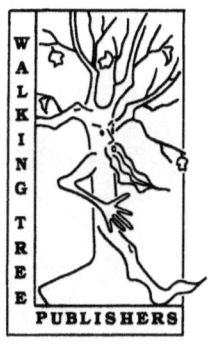

Walking Tree Publishers was founded in 1997 as a forum for publication of material (books, videos, CDs, etc.) related to Tolkien and Middle-earth studies. Manuscripts and project proposals can be submitted to the board of editors (please include an SAE):

Walking Tree Publishers
CH-3052 Zollikofen
Switzerland
e-mail: walkingtree@go.to
http://go.to/walkingtree

Publications:

Cormarë Series

News from the Shire and Beyond. Studies on Tolkien.
Edited by Peter Buchs and Thomas Honegger. Zurich and Berne 2004. Reprint. 1st edition 1997. (Cormarë Series 1)

Root and Branch. Approaches Towards Understanding Tolkien.
Edited by Thomas Honegger. Zurich and Berne 2005. Reprint. 1st edition 1999. (Cormarë Series 2)

Richard Sturch. *Four Christian Fantasists. A Study of the Fantastic Writings of George MacDonald, Charles Williams, C. S. Lewis and J.R.R. Tolkien.*
Zurich and Berne 2001. (Cormarë Series 3)

Tolkien in Translation.
Edited by Thomas Honegger. Zurich and Berne 2003. (Cormarë Series 4)

Mark T. Hooker. *Tolkien Through Russian Eyes.* Zurich and Berne 2003. (Cormarë Series 5)

Translating Tolkien: Text and Film.
Edited by Thomas Honegger. Zurich and Berne 2004. (Cormarë Series 6)

Christopher Garbowski. *Recovery and Transcendence for the Contemporary Mythmaker: The Spiritual Dimension in the Works of J.R.R. Tolkien.*
Zurich and Berne 2004. Reprint. 1st edition by Marie Curie Sklodowska University Press, Lublin 2000. (Cormarë Series 7)

Tales of Yore Series

Kay Woollard. *The Terror of Tatty Walk. A Frightener.* CD and booklet. Zurich and Berne 2000. (Tales of Yore 1)

Kay Woollard, *Wilmot's Very Strange Stone or What came of building "snobbits".* CD and booklet. Zurich and Berne 2001. (Tales of Yore 2)

www.ingramcontent.com/pod-product-compliance
Lightning Source LLC
Chambersburg PA
CBHW070742160426
43192CB00009B/1540